ISIS, IRAN, ISRAEL

MARK HITCHCOCK

HARVEST HOUSE PUBLISHERS
EUGENE, OREGON

Cover by Aesthetic Soup

Cover photo © Benjamin Haas / Shutterstock

Published in association with William K. Jensen Literary Agency, 119 Bampton Court, Eugene, Oregon 97404.

ISIS, IRAN, ISRAEL
Copyright © 2013, 2016 by Mark Hitchcock
Published by Harvest House Publishers
Eugene, Oregon 97402
www.harvesthousepublishers.com

ISBN 978-0-7369-6871-3 (pbk.)
ISBN 978-0-7369-6916-1 (eBook)

The Library of Congress has cataloged the earlier edition as follows:
    Hitchcock, Mark, 1959-
    Iran and Israel / Mark Hitchcock.
        p. cm.
    ISBN 978-0-7369-5334-4 (pbk.)
    1. Islam—Iran. 2. Iran—Social conditions—1997- 3. Iran—Politics and government—1997- 4. Iran—Economic conditions—1997- 5. Nuclear weapons—Iran. 6. Iran—Foreign relations—Israel. 7. Israel—Foreign relations—Iran. 8. Bible—Prophecies. I. Title.
    BP63.I68H58 2013
    220.1'5—dc23
                                                                            2012031798

To Tim LaHaye

Thank you for your friendship and encouragement.
You are a blessing to me and my family and
the body of Christ.

Contents

CHAPTER 1

Middle East Meltdown

"Our world is on fire, and man without God will never be able to control the flames. The demons of hell have been let loose. The fires of passion, greed, hate, and lust are sweeping the world. We seem to be plunging madly toward Armageddon... The world has been in flames before, but only in a limited sense. Today our world is a common neighborhood, all of it reachable in mere hours by physical flight and in seconds over the airwaves. This accessibility increases the spread of tension and dissension. Thus when the fires of war and lawlessness break out, they leap the national boundaries and cultural differences to become major conflagrations. The whole world is filled with riots, demonstrations, threats, wars... This is the generation destined to live in the midst of crisis, danger, fear, and death. We are like a people under sentence of death, waiting for the date to be set. We sense that something is about to happen."[1]

Billy Graham, *World Aflame* (1965)

*"This is a time of global transformation. We are
essentially seeing a new world order evolving
and being built. I don't think we've seen such
a time since right after World War II."*[2]

Chuck Hagel, U.S. Defense Secretary

The Middle East is in meltdown. The horrifying images on our TV screens have become commonplace. Brutal killers are wreaking havoc, and the atrocities are unspeakable. The vacuum left by the retreat of American leadership in the Middle East has been filled by some pretty bad actors. Desperate political, military, and humanitarian crises have resulted. The disarray and danger is mushrooming and spreading out to the entire world. What's currently unfolding is nothing short of a region-wide disintegration with Syria, Iraq, Libya, Afghanistan, and Yemen in varying forms of chaos and dysfunction along with a rising Iran with nuclear ambitions, a re-emerging Russia, and the ruthless threat from ISIS. The tiny nation of Israel is at the epicenter of all the upheaval. Israel is the ultimate prize for radical Islam. America remains a coveted target for terror. A bigger mess and greater danger can hardly be imagined. And the danger is proliferating. How much worse will it get?

A summary of just one month of terror graphically captures the growing picture.

Paris. Baghdad. Beirut. Sharm el-Sheikh. Ankara. In striking these cities in the last several weeks, the Islamic State group has made it clear that it's raising the stakes. On Nov. 13, the same day as the Paris attacks, the jihadi terrorist organization carried out an attack that claimed 26 lives in Baghdad. On Nov. 12, bombings in Beirut left 43 dead. A month earlier, 100 Turks were killed after a bombing targeted a rally in Ankara. Meanwhile, the attack on the Russian Metrojet flights on Oct. 31 killed all 244 on board.[3]

Planes are falling from the sky. ISIS is on the march. Major cities are being struck by terror attacks with vicious threats of more to come. Syria is embroiled in a grinding civil war. Lawless Libya is a fertile breeding ground for jihadists. Terror is spreading like a brush fire.

The ISIS-directed and synchronized slaughter in Paris gripped the world. The West is paralyzed by fear. Iran is uncoiling its tentacles into Iraq and Syria and covertly pursuing nukes even as the controversial, flimsy nuclear deal goes into effect. Russia is busily moving troops, tanks, and airpower into Syria, expanding its influence. Few believe Russia and Iran will ever leave Syria.

At the center of much of the turmoil is Islam. Of course, as everyone should know by now, most Muslims are not terrorists or jihadists. Political pundits remind us of this over and over again. Radical Islam is a small but growing subset of the global Muslim population.

However, there's more to the story. A further subset of
radical Islam is apocalyptic Islam, and the armies of the
apocalypse are fomenting Armageddon. As Joel Rosenberg notes, "Indeed, for the first time in human history,
the top leaders of not just one nation state but two—Iran
and the Islamic State—are being driven by Islamic eschatology, or End Times theology."[4] Two entire nation-states
are currently driven by an apocalyptic, genocidal ideology fueled by their view that the end of days is at hand.
These nation-states are ISIS and Iran. One is Sunni Muslim (ISIS) and the other is Shiite Muslim (Iran), but both
are fired by a common belief that they are harbingers of
the end of days. Driven by eschatology and millenarian
fervor, they view themselves as laying down the welcome
mat for their messiah (the Mahdi). For them, the mission
and momentum is unstoppable. The end is here.

Rising out of the wreckage of Iraq and Syria, ISIS
has brashly declared the formation of a proto-caliphate.
Their fanatical leader Abu Bakr al-Baghdadi announced
its birth on June 29, 2014. For ISIS this marked a major
milestone. "The revival of the caliphate is the launching
pad for a global battlefield."[5] Prophecy is critical to ISIS,
which accepts the word of the Prophet and the hadith,
or sayings, attributed to him literally and without question. Prophecy provides ISIS with the glue of theological
certainty. And according to those prophecies, the Islamic
armies will ultimately conquer Jerusalem and Rome.[6] We
must never forget that the final goal is the destruction
of Israel and a global caliphate. Israel is in the crosshairs
of radical and apocalyptic Islam. Everything else is just

a stepping-stone on the road to Jerusalem. Abu Bakr al-Baghdadi, the head of ISIS, warned Israel:

> The Jews thought we forgot Palestine and that they had distracted us from it. Not at all, Jews. We did not forget Palestine for a moment. With the help of Allah, we will not forget it...The pioneers of the jihadist fighters will surround you on a day that you think is distant and we know is close. We are getting closer every day. You will never find comfort in Palestine, Jews. Palestine will not be your land or your home, but it will be a graveyard for you. Allah assembled you in Palestine so that the Muslims kill you, so that you may hide behind stones and trees (a Muslim tradition regarding the killing of Jews).[7]

Israel is the goal, but anyone who stands in the way of the caliphate is a target.

THE TICKING TIME BOMB OF TERROR

The distant threat of terror now seems to have jumped into everyone's life. Years ago, America was shaken to the core by the 9/11 attacks. European nations have been targeted multiple times and appear to still be marked with a bull's-eye. America anxiously waits for the other shoe to drop.

Army psychiatrist Nidal Hasan, inflamed by radical Islam, opened fire at Ft. Hood in Texas on November 5, 2009, killing thirteen people. On April 15, 2013, three people were murdered and dozens more were wounded and maimed at the Boston Marathon massacre perpetrated by two brothers committed to Islamic radicalism. Then, seemingly out of nowhere on December 2, 2015, ISIS killers slaughtered fourteen people in San Bernardino, California, and wounded twenty-one others—the worst terror attack on U.S. soil since 9/11. The radicalized couple who carried out the attack swore allegiance to ISIS and its leader on Facebook.

In the wake of the steady stream of attacks and threats, everyone wonders where the terror will strike next. New terror threats spring up with all-too-frequent regularity. The cascade of recent events has highlighted a reality most Westerners would rather close their eyes to: We have vulnerabilities—major ones. No one seems safe anymore— anywhere. As the attacks increase, calls for a stronger response will resonate with Americans and Europeans weary of waiting for the next explosion or hail of gunfire. As the pressure ratchets up, the divide will grow. Many voices are calling for boots on the ground in Syria and Iraq to battle ISIS. Time will tell if, and how, ISIS can be slowed or stopped.

Iran's Increase

Added to the shocking acts of terror by ISIS is Iran's relentless pursuit of nuclear weapons and its ever-expanding tentacles of terror. Iran has publicly, repeatedly declared its intent to obliterate Israel. Iran has signed the nuclear deal, but at the same time its leader regularly chants "Death to America," and its supreme leader gleefully threatens that Israel won't exist in 25 years. Iran and Israel have been locked in a shadow war for decades since the Islamic revolution in 1979. Israel has assassinated numerous key Iranian scientists to slow down Iran's nuclear pursuits (although Israel never acknowledges this fact). Israel has infected the Iranian nuclear program with numerous computer viruses in further attempts to derail the nuclear train. In recent days Iran has agreed to a nuclear deal with P5 + 1 nations (United States, United Kingdom, Russia, France, China, and Germany) that gives them access to $150 billion in cash, removal of crippling sanctions, and the right to have a nuclear program.

Few believe Iran will live up to its end of the nuclear deal and that cheating will mean its hot pursuit of nuclear weapons will continue. Fully aware that Israel might launch a preemptive strike on its nuclear production facilities, Iran has gone to great lengths to make its underground nuclear megacomplex as impenetrable as possible.

To add a further line of defense, Iran finances and trains Hezbollah fighters in Lebanon who have amassed thousands of rockets and a formidable terrorist army on Israel's northern border. Hamas, which runs Gaza on Israel's border, is another Iranian surrogate. These two Iranian proxies—Hezbollah and Hamas—that live on Israel's borders are a constant irritant and deterrent against any aggression by Israel against Iran. Nevertheless, when Iran breaks the conditions of the fragile nuclear deal, will the United States or Israel feel compelled to launch a pre-emptive strike against Iran to end the threat?

THE LOOMING CRISIS

The steady surge in the pace, perplexity, and problems of modern life has given the entire world a sense of looming crisis. ISIS is unleashing its chaos and cruelty in the Middle East and North Africa. Iran is racing toward the nuclear finish line in spite of its acceptance of the nuclear deal.

At the same time, the Russian bear is on the move: first, Crimea, then Ukraine and Syria. Russian troops are now perched on Israel's northern border. Russian dominance has reemerged with a vengeance. What could never have been imagined is right before our eyes. How will Russia continue to exert its influence in the Middle East? Will Iran violate the nuclear deal and unleash nuclear jihad? What's out there beyond the headlights in the darkness?

By any measure, the Middle East today is a powder keg that seems ready to explode at any time. How long can world tensions be kept in check? How long until the lid blows sky-high? How long can the struggle against radical Islamic terror be restrained from descending into a global bloodbath? Modern man's ability to wreak havoc and destruction is almost boundless: biological and chemical agents, dirty bombs, and WMDs are harder and harder to keep out of the hands of fanatical terrorists.

Our world appears to be moving toward a colossal crisis—a decisive showdown in the Middle East. Is it possible the prophets of doom are right? Could the escalating crisis in the Middle East be part of something even bigger? Could it be the prelude—the buildup—for the final events of this age predicted long ago in the pages of the Bible? Or could it be a buildup to the start of the Tribulation? Is the world racing toward the end of days? More than twenty years ago, prophecy scholar Dr. John Walvoord noted that the first key to the Armageddon countdown is that "the Middle East must become the number one crisis in the world."[8] There's no doubt that the Middle East is the number one hot spot in the world. That piece of the prophetic puzzle is now firmly in place.

ACCORDING TO PLANS

Years ago I used to watch the TV program *The A-Team* with my nephew. It was his favorite program. Each episode followed a fairly simple, similar pattern. The members of the A-Team formulated a plan to rescue somebody or even themselves. Often at the end of the episode one of the main characters would say, "Don't you just love it when a plan comes together?"

In a world gone mad, we must remember that God has a sovereign plan that is coming together. God's rescue plan has already come into effect with the first coming of Jesus Christ to earth, but the Bible predicts He will come again at the end of history for the final act of rescue. Piece

by piece God's final plan seems to be coming together
to pave the way for Christ's return. Israel is back in her
ancient homeland as predicted often in biblical prophecy. Nations are moving into their prophesied places as
foretold more than 2500 years ago by the prophet Ezekiel.
World events and today's headlines bear a remarkable correspondence with the end-time scenario in Scripture.

As shocking and saddening as world events are today,
they should not surprise us in light of the Bible's end-
times prophecies. The Hebrew prophets of the Old Testament and the New Testament apostles predicted many
future events in vivid, often precise detail, including the
rise and fall of every major world empire that left its mark
on the Middle East. Some of their predictions came
true within a few years or within their lifetimes. Now
it appears that the stage is being set for many of their
astounding unfulfilled prophecies to come to pass at any
time.

Jesus Himself, Israel's premier prophet, quoted from
the Old Testament prophets—often adding interpre-
tive comments and detailed predictions of His own. The
prophecies of Jesus have been fully corroborated by the
test of time. Jesus' prediction of the fall of Jerusalem
(Luke 21:20-24) was vividly fulfilled in AD 70 when
Titus and his Roman legions destroyed Jerusalem and lev-
eled the second Jewish temple. Jesus also accurately predicted the scattering of the Jews into all nations, and the
persecution, survival, and global growth of the church.

About six million Jews are settled in the land of Israel

today, almost forty percent of the Jews in the world, and their return is one of the most frequent Old Testament prophecies (Ezekiel 37). Consistent with these prophets, Jesus saw a time when Israel would be reestablished as a nation after their worldwide dispersion (see Matthew 24:15-20). This prophecy has been dramatically fulfilled in recent history with the rebirth of the modern state of Israel in 1948. Since that time Jerusalem, the "city of peace," has been constantly under duress from its surrounding nations. Time and again Israel has found itself in a dangerous, diplomatic tug-of-war just as the ancient prophets predicted (Zechariah 12:1-3). In His prophetic discourse just a few days before His death, Jesus outlined the blueprint of the final days on earth before His return. Jesus forewarned His followers to watch Jerusalem for signs of the approaching end of the age (Matthew 24). We are wise to study His blueprint.

THE SEARCH FOR ANSWERS

Everywhere we look, people are wondering what on earth is going on. The fear and anxiety is palpable. Even people with little interest in the Bible or end-time scenarios are quietly asking questions—wondering if the world is getting near closing time. Believers, too, have all kinds of questions. They are solemn, searching questions. If we are on the home stretch of the church age, what will happen next? Where is history headed? What are the final events of world history as the end of the age draws near?

Do today's headlines relate to these events? Can we find a certain word about the future?

The Bible is certainly the best place—the only place—to look for sure answers. The hundreds of fulfilled prophecies in Scripture, which span many centuries, can be put to the test by observing their literal, precise fulfillment. Because of its proven track record of 100 percent accuracy 100 percent of the time and the turmoil in today's headlines, both believers and skeptics are re-examining the end-time prophecies in Scripture, especially the ancient prophecy in Ezekiel 38–39 that foretells an end-time invasion of Israel by a coalition of nations from every direction.

This is a book about the Bible and current events, but more particularly, it is about how current events point toward what's coming in the future. As we will see, the Bible doesn't answer every question we have or give us every detail about the future, but it does provide the template for where we're headed. The Bible is a revelation of the past, present, and future—not just of individuals but also of nations and the movements of history. It is the prism through which we can see what's coming and make sense of what's happening today.

In the prophecies of Scripture, I believe it is possible to discover clues that point to where we are in God's prophetic program and the predicted events that may occur very soon. The Bible, and the Bible alone, can answer the pressing questions on the minds of so many people—questions about today, questions about tomorrow. In this book we will seek to answer many of the compelling questions people are asking in light of increasingly turbulent world events.

Are we on the road to Armageddon?

What can we expect in the days to come?

Where did ISIS come from?

What do ISIS and Islam believe about the end times?

Is the rise of ISIS mentioned in Bible prophecy?

Does ISIS have any biblical significance?

What does the Bible say about the future of the Middle East?

Will the Middle East go up in the flames of a regional war?

What role will Iran play?

What about Russia?

What will happen to America?

How should we respond as the world seems to be on the verge of disaster?

My hope is this book will help answer these pressing questions for you and give you hope for both your own future and the future of this world.

CHAPTER 2

MetastISIS

*"The Islamic State, a.k.a. ISIS, is the wealthiest, most
successful, and most dangerous terror group in the
world—and the most mysterious...one jihad terror
group has outdone them all by actually establishing that
Islamic State—and embarking upon a reign of terror
unmatched in recent memory—rivaling the atrocities
of Hitler, Stalin, Mao, and Pol Pot...The Islamic State
is nothing less than the foremost evil force of our time."*[1]

Robert Spencer, *The Complete Infidel's Guide to ISIS*

*"In some ways, it's an unprecedented threat
environment that we're facing."*[2]

John Carlin, assistant attorney general
for national security

In the spring of 2015, a group from our church traveled to Israel for a tour of the Holy Land. On our final day in Galilee (northern Israel), we journeyed to the

Israel-Syria border on the Golan Heights. We stood a few hundred yards from the fence that marks the border, realizing this barrier divides two totally different worlds. The people in Syria are trapped in a brutal civil war pitting the regime troops of Bashar al-Assad against more than 30 rebel factions, including several Islamic terror groups, most notably ISIS.

While we were there at the border, suddenly several loud explosions thundered, shattering the silence. A few minutes later more blasts shook the ground under our feet. Our Israeli guide told us the shelling we heard was ISIS. He said that a few weeks earlier he had brought a group right to the place we were standing, and a full-scale skirmish broke out in the town just over the Syrian border. He told how they watched the firefight in horror for several minutes as ISIS barbarians slaughtered citizens and eventually took the town.

As I looked across the border into that deserted town, listened to the story of its capture by ISIS, and heard the shelling just a few miles away, the brutal reality of ISIS became personal. I stood there safe and comfortable, soon traveling back home to the United States, but saw a town just a few hundred yards away that languished under the dark shadow of the black flag of ISIS. The chilling scenes of brutal beheadings, chaotic carnage, cruel crucifixions, cities under siege, and apocalyptic anticipation were suddenly right in front of me. I will never forget that chilling, hollow feeling I had for the desperate people trapped behind that fence.

Fast-forward to November 2015. We all watched in horror as a sinister synchronized attack struck Paris and paralyzed an entire nation. The terrorists, we quickly learned, were ISIS operatives. They called the Paris attacks the "first of the storm." Belgium was on high alert for days under the cloud of a threatened attack. Headlines around the world focused on ISIS.

"How the ISIS fight went global," cnn.com (November 16, 2015)

"Feinstein: 'I Have Never Been More Concerned. I Read the Intelligence Faithfully. ISIS Is Not Contained. ISIS Is Expanding,'" real clearpolitics.com (November 16, 2015)

"Russia Says Bomb Downed Plane in Egypt and Intensifies Attacks on ISIS," nytimes.com (November 17, 2015)

"ISIS claims responsibility for Paris massacre," *New York Daily News* (November 14, 2015)

Then less than a month later, ISIS came to America. On December 2, 2015, a sleeper cell husband and wife, radicalized by ISIS, slaughtered 14 people and wounded many more at a workplace Christmas party. ISIS took to Twitter to gloat over the atrocity, saying, "Three lions made us proud. They are still alive. California streets are full with soldiers with heavy weapons. The United States is burning #America_Burning #Takbir."[3] ISIS followers boasted this event would "let America know a new era." Tragically, ISIS was right. A new era of terror is now upon us. According to the Justice Department, U.S. prosecutors have charged more than 80 people with terror-related offenses since the start of 2014—at least 60 alone in 2015, with the lion's share of the cases related to ISIS.[4] Terror plots continued to unfold.

> "Rochester man linked to ISIS planned New Year's Eve Machete Attack," NBC News (December 31, 2015)

> "German police evacuate 2 train stations in Munich, warn public over ISIS suicide attack threat," RT.com (December 31, 2015)

> "ISIS terrorism topped the news in 2015," Fox News (December 31, 2015)

ISIS Is Born

ISIS—just four letters. But what these letters embody is almost impossible to get one's head around. ISIS stands for *Islamic State of Iraq and Syria*, but it goes by different names. ISIL refers to *Islamic State of Iraq and the Levant* (*Levant* is an old term for the geographical area that today is Israel, Syria, Lebanon, and Jordan). Sometimes the group is simply called the Islamic State. Whatever moniker it bears, the result is the same. ISIS is on the move, swallowing up town after town, slaughtering "infidels," declaring the establishment of a caliphate, and heralding the end of days. Where did this evil entity come from? What do they want?

ISIS began as a splinter group or "franchise" of Al-Qaeda in Iraq. At the beginning it was simply known as Al-Qaeda in Iraq, but the cancer of Al-Qaeda quickly metastasized into ISIS. Its first leader was Abu Musab al-Zarqawi. The brand of terror they practice is set apart from other Al-Qaeda affiliates in several ways. First, they target other Muslims (Shiites) as well as non-Muslims. Any person who is a non-Sunni Muslim is fair game. ISIS has sought and succeeded in creating a sectarian civil war between Sunnis and Shiites in Iraq. Saddam Hussein was a Sunni who dominated a predominantly Shia population in Iraq. When he was deposed, many Shiites saw this as a time for payback. ISIS fed this sentiment and fueled the sectarian divide.

Second, the tactics and methods of ISIS are horrific and gruesome, including beheading, rampant rape, chopping off hands and feet, and even crucifixion. The Islamic State's presence in the Middle East cannot be described as anything other than a reign of terror. The motto of ISIS is "Come or kill," which means come join us in the death struggle in the Middle East or kill where you are. Wherever they're found, ISIS leaves a trail of terror.

Third, not satisfied with terror alone, ISIS wants territory. Their goal is to conquer and consolidate—to take land and hold it. ISIS wants a caliphate and they want it now; they have no patience to wait. ISIS sees itself as "following in the footsteps of the first great Arab conquests, and its attainments are similar to those of the early Arab conquerors."[5] The singular achievement of ISIS, distinct from all other jihadist groups, is "that it has managed to conquer and hold territory."[6]

A chain of at least three events converged to birth ISIS to develop and then mushroom into the diabolical force it is today. First, ISIS came into being during the day of the U.S. presence in Iraq, and was propelled to power when the U.S. withdrawal from Iraq left a vacuum that they were quick to fill.

Second, in 2006, al-Zarqawi, the founder of ISIS, was killed in a targeted air attack. Another leader took over and declared the creation of the Islamic State of Iraq (ISI). Syria was later added to the title, and ISI became ISIS. The Islamic State then stagnated for a few years, but that all changed in 2010 with the rise of another new leader, Abu Bakr al-Baghdadi. He stoked ISIS into the bloodthirsty brigade it has become.

Third, around that same time, the rise of ISIS was spurred by the Arab Spring that began in Tunisia. All over the Middle East and North Africa, dictatorial governments were toppled, including the removal of Hosni Mubarek in Egypt and Muammar Gadhafi in Libya. Al-Baghdadi, the leader of ISIS, brought his group into Syria in 2011 to face off against the forces of Bashar al-Assad in Syria in an attempt to remove him. ISIS forces captured the Syrian city of Dabiq, which they believe is the site of the final great battle at the end of the age. Dabiq is the place Muhammad is supposed to have predicted where the armies of Islam will face the armies of "Rome" for the final battle that will inaugurate the end times and usher in the triumph of Islam.

Taking Dabiq was a major milestone for ISIS and their doomsday vision. In 2013, ISIS overran the city of Raqqa in Syria and turned it into its de facto capital. Some have described the city as a "giant prison" where the populace lives under draconian laws. "Women are banned from walking the street unaccompanied by a man and must adhere to strict Muslim dress code. They live with no electricity or hot water and are prevented from working...In the once relaxed city, offenders are held in cages, decapitated, have hands cut off, and lashed with whips in public."[7]

Beginning in 2014, Al-Qaeda severed all ties with ISIS, and ISIS "supplanted its former master, al-Qaeda, to lead the global jihadist movement."[8] ISIS wasted no time in launching its initial offensive in Iraq and quickly established a beachhead. Swallowing village after village, ISIS unleashed an unparalleled campaign of terror. They took Iraq's second-largest city, Mosul, and Tikrit in June 2014. And they seized control of Ramadi, the second-largest city in western Iraq, in May 2015.

The black-and-white flag of ISIS is among the most feared symbols in the world. The flowing Arabic letters on the flag cite the words of the Shahada: "There is no God but Allah, Muhammad is the messenger of Allah."

The seal of Muhammad is positioned at the bottom of the flag. The bold aim is to establish a caliphate—an Islamic state—across the Middle East with forced imposition of strict Sharia law. ISIS won't rest until the black flag flies across the entire Middle East and the end of days arrives.

CALIPHATE REBORN

The last Islamic caliphate, the Ottoman Empire, lasted for centuries but eroded over time and finally collapsed during the first two decades of the twentieth century. On June 29, 2014, the leader of ISIS announced the creation of a caliphate (Islamic State) that erased all national borders, effectively making its leader the self-appointed authority over the global Muslim population. Suddenly the caliphate was reborn, and ISIS believes prophecy was fulfilled when this took place.

The caliphate is central to the strategy of ISIS and their end-of-days ideology. For them, the end of days is at hand, and the caliphate is a precursor to the advent of their messiah. The appeal of ISIS and the caliphate is so magnetic and irresistible to young Muslims that by the end of May 2015, nearly 30,000 Muslims from 115 nations had joined ISIS in Iraq and Syria, with an additional 5,000 joining the wing of ISIS in Libya.[9]

ISIS is now in multiple nations and holds territory equivalent to the size of the United Kingdom. They have spread into Afghanistan, Libya, Yemen, and Egypt, but Libya is the only other place besides Iraq and Syria where

ISIS holds territory. Experts fear that ISIS cells in Europe
and the United States are biding their time for the next
outbreak of terror. Intelligence and law enforcement
agencies are on high alert. Every means of information-
gathering is being employed, but because of limited
resources, not every lead and not every suspect can be followed. As the saying goes, "We have to be right 100 percent of the time, while the terrorists only have to be right
once." The cancer is spreading even as you read these
words, and it's driven by an ideology that is very difficult
to quash.

ISIS, Inc.

The proto-caliphate has found many ways to
finance its brutality. "They leave no source of money
untouched—this is their lifeblood."[10] ISIS has been very
effective at keeping its coffers full. "It helped that the
Islamic State was able to gain control of several reliable—
and immense—sources of wealth and ultimately to
become the richest jihad terror group the world has ever
known."[11] The emerging caliphate is funded from several
major sources. One major financial supply line is looting. "The Islamic State looted nearly $500 million from
the banks in the city of Mosul alone."[12] ISIS also steals
and sells priceless antiquities on the black market (that is,
the ones they don't destroy or raze). Extortion and kid-
napping for ransom provides another steady source of
income. The U.S. Treasury Department estimates that

ISIS took in $20 million in ransom payments in 2014. Donors from more than 40 nations have stepped forward to finance ISIS. In 2013 and 2014 alone, more than $40 million was received in donations. The militants have also made more than $500 million selling cheap oil on the black market to Syria, with some of it making its way to Turkey and Kurdish areas. The current estimate sets the monthly income from oil at $40 million.

Looting, donations, ransom payments, and oil are all bringing large sums of money to ISIS, but another often-overlooked bonanza for the Islamic State is taxes. As Erika Solomon and Sam Jones note, "Even under jihadi rule, death and taxes remain the two great certainties of life."[13] ISIS holds one-half of the territory in Syria and one-third of Iraq, which provide a large swath of territory to terrorize and tax.

With these sources of income, ISIS is financially formidable. Taking all these various sources into account, the best estimate is that ISIS currently takes in about $6 million a day.

THE GREAT DIVIDE: SUNNIS AND SHIITES

Before we transition to the next chapter to focus on the end-of-days ideology of ISIS, a very brief bit of historical background about Islam is helpful for understanding the current Middle East showdown. Muslims are primarily split into two groups: Sunnis and Shiites. About 85-90 percent are Sunni, and 10-15 percent are Shiite. The divide between the two groups ultimately comes down to the issue of who was the rightful successor to Muhammad after his death. *Sunni* means "custom or tradition," and adherents to this strain of Islam maintain Muhammad's successor was Abu Bakr, who was not a blood relative of Muhammad. He was favored because of his personal piety and exceptional ability to communicate the beliefs and values of Islam. For Sunnis, he was the legitimate heir.

Shiite Muslims trace their roots back to Muhammad's son-in-law and cousin, Ali ibn Abi Talib, as the rightful successor. They believe that all future successors must hail from the line of Ali and his wife Fatima (Muhammad's daughter). Therein lies the basis for the split.

Bringing this to the contemporary scene, Iran is a Shiite nation, and Iraq has a Shiite majority. The only other Middle Eastern nation with a Shiite majority is Bahrain. All the others are Sunni majority. ISIS and Al-Qaeda are Sunni terrorist groups. Nevertheless, in spite of their differences, both Sunnis and Shiites hold to an apocalyptic scenario for the future. In groups like ISIS, the apocalyptic element is front and center.

Sunnis and Shiites both believe in an Islamic redeemer called the *Mahdi*—a messiah-like figure who will be joined by Jesus to rule the earth before the day of judgment. But there is one major difference between the groups: Sunnis are waiting for the Mahdi to appear in the future, while the Shiites teach he is already here but hidden (they call him the hidden Imam). Shiites also believe

there have been 12 successors to the prophet Muhammad. Ali was the first in this line, and the twelfth and
final imam is Muhammad ibn al-Hasan, also known as
Muhammad al-Mahdi.[14]

We will learn more about the Twelfth Imam and Iran
in chapter 6. Now let's dig deeper into the millennial
madness that motivates ISIS.

FAST FACTS ABOUT ISIS

- *ISIS* stands for Islamic State in Iraq and Syria. Also
  known as Islamic State in Iraq and the Levant (ISIL)
  and Islamic State (IS).

- Started as an Al-Qaeda splinter group.

- Led by Abu Bakr al-Baghdadi; also goes by the name
  Abu Du'a. After ISIS declared the creation of the so-
  called Islamic State, he began using the name Al-
  Khalifah Ibrahim, and now goes by that name with his
  followers.

- Currently based in Syria.

- De facto capital is the city of Raqqa (pop. 500,000) in
  northern Syria.

- Goal is to create an Islamic state called a caliphate
  across Iraq, Syria, and beyond.

- Enforces Sharia law to establish a society that mirrors
  the ancient past of the region.

- Notorious for brutality and barbaric acts—killing dozens of people at a time, carrying out public executions, crucifixions, and embracing a theology of rape.

- Employs modern tools like social media to promote reactionary politics and religious fundamentalism.

- Destroys holy sites and valuable antiquities as their leaders propagate a return to the early days of Islam.

- Controls more than 34,000 square miles in Syria and Iraq, from the Mediterranean coast to south of Baghdad (a swath of territory about the size of the United Kingdom) that includes 8 million people.

ISIS: TIME LINE OF TERROR

- **October 2006:** Jihadist groups within the Iraqi insurgency, including some affiliated with Al Qaeda in Iraq, establish the Islamic State of Iraq, and vow in a video recording to plant "the flag of the state of Islam."

- **July 2013–January 2014:** Activists report that ISIS is gradually seizing control of smaller cities in northern Syria. In January, it takes control of Raqqa, its first capture of a major city.

- **January 2014:** ISIS marches into Fallujah and parts of Ramadi in Iraq, both in Anbar province, the Sunni heartland.

- **February 2014:** Al-Qaeda officially cuts all ties with ISIS.

- **June 2014:** ISIS launches a lightning offensive and captures vast expanses of both Iraq and Syria, including Mosul, the second-largest city in Iraq, and Saddam Hussein's hometown, Tikrit.

- **June 29, 2014:** ISIS leaders boldly announce they have established a caliphate.

- **August 19, 2014:** ISIS releases a video depicting the beheading of James Foley, an American journalist they held hostage, and warns of more to come if President Obama does not call off air strikes carried out on them. More public beheadings and atrocities continue.

- **November 2015:** ISIS brings down a Russian charter jet in the Sinai; kills dozens in Ankara, Turkey, and Beirut, Lebanon in suicide bombings; orchestrates a terror attack in Paris; and paralyzes the Belgian capital, Brussels, for days with threats of an attack.[15]

CHAPTER 3

ISIS Apocalypse

"The Islamic State is no mere collection of psychopaths. It is a religious group with carefully considered beliefs, among them that it is a key agent of the coming apocalypse...Its rise to power is less like the triumph of the Muslim Brotherhood in Egypt (a group whose leaders the Islamic State considers apostates) than like the realization of a dystopian alternate reality in which David Koresh or Jim Jones survived to wield absolute power over not just a few hundred people, but some 8 million."[1]

Graeme Wood, "What ISIS Really Wants," *The Atlantic*

"ISIS makes no secret of its ultimate ambition: A global caliphate secured through a global war."[2]

Tim Lister, "What Does ISIS Really Want?" CNN

In 1979, a movie was released that was instantly destined to be a classic. In fact, some still claim it is one of the greatest movies of all time. Set in Vietnam during the war, the title was apropos and arresting—*Apocalypse Now*. With a star-studded cast it told the dark story of Captain Benjamin L. Willard's secret mission to assassinate a renegade colonel named Walter E. Kurtz, who was believed to be insane. The group Kurtz led was depraved and debauched. When Willard reached his destination, he encountered a horrific, surreal scene with dead bodies and severed heads littering the compound. Kurtz ruled a gruesome death cult.

One haunting scene near the end of the movie features Colonel Kurtz quietly, eerily whispering the words, "The horror, the horror." ISIS strikes me as a modern version of *Apocalypse Now*. ISIS is a renegade, rogue group, insane in its thirst for blood and firmly convinced it plays a key role in the grand climax of the ages. It is willing to do anything to bring to fruition its dystopian vision of an apocalyptic bloodbath. Australian Prime Minister Tony Abbott aptly dubbed ISIS an "apocalyptic death cult" whose aim is "to have heads on stakes."[3] ISIS's version of jihad is volcanic.

ARMY OF THE APOCALYPSE

While many factors may play a role in the rise of ISIS, the end of days is the linchpin of ISIS ideology and propaganda. It drives everything. ISIS believes it plays a key role in ushering in the end of days. The Islamic State was proclaimed on October 15, 2006, and the announcement was based on a precise apocalyptic schedule.[4] ISIS

believes the Mahdi will be preceded by an Islamic caliphate and views itself as the restoration of the caliphate—
and thus, the harbinger of the end times.

Will McCants says, "When the Islamic State was
established in 2006, the group's chief judge at the time
said the group was created because they believed the
Muslim savior, or Mahdi, was going to come any day,
and the Islamic State had to be established to help him
fight the infidels.[5] Here are a few insightful remarks that
give us an open window into the apocalyptic vision of
ISIS.

> All Muslims acknowledge that God is the only
> one who knows the future. But they also agree
> that he has offered us a peek at it, in the Koran
> and in narrations of the Prophet. The Islamic
> State differs from nearly every other current
> jihadist movement in believing that it is written
> into God's script as a central character. It is in
> this casting that the Islamic State is most boldly
> distinctive from its predecessors, and clearest in
> the religious nature of its mission.[6]

> [ISIS] considers itself a harbinger of—and
> headline player in—the imminent end of the
> world.[7]

> The Islamic State believes it's on a "divine
> mission" to lure unbelievers into Syria for an
> Armageddon-like battle. They don't see being
> way too brutal as a bad thing...Brutality is

working for them. They don't see taking over
the world as overstretching. This is part of the
divine mission...the more the West strikes in
Syria, it only builds into the narrative that the
end is coming.[8]

The Islamic State is thus positioning itself
as the harbinger of the end times—of the final
and decisive battle between the Muslims and
the enemies of Allah, from which the Muslims
will emerge victorious, after which peace—the
peace of total Sharia adherence—will prevail
over all the earth.[9]

Abu Bakr al-Baghdadi, the chief of ISIS, believes the
gathering of nations against ISIS in Syria and Iraq for one
great final battle is happening today. For him, what's happening in the Middle East is the setup for the final great
battle.

To help us better understand the current strain of
apocalyptic Islam embodied in ISIS and Iran, here are
some fundamental features of Islamic eschatology:

• that the End of Days have arrived

• that the Islamic messiah known as the "Mahdi"
  will appear at any moment

• that when the Mahdi appears, he will rule the
  entire Earth

- that Jesus will also return to Earth, but not as the Messiah, or Savior, or Son of God, but as the deputy to the Mahdi

- that Jesus will force all Jews, Christians and other so-called "infidels" to convert to Islam or be executed

- that the way to hasten the arrival and full establishment of the global Islamic kingdom or "caliphate" is to annihilate Jews and Christians, and specifically to annihilate Israel (which they call the "Little Satan" in their eschatology), and the United States (which they call the "Great Satan")

- that time is very short, and they must move decisively because soon each Muslim will face the Mahdi face to face and be brought into judgment if they have not faithfully followed the Mahdi's orders.[10]

Here's a summary of the Islamic view of the end:

> Mahdi will lead Muslims to a great victory against the Christian Romans (i.e. All the white Europeans including the Americans). This great war is called al-Malhamah al-Kubrah or Armageddon. It will end up with a great victory to Muslims against Romans after six years.

Muslims will take over their capital Rome (this can be any city). In the seventh year, the Antichrist will appear and a greater war will start between Jews and Muslims for 40 days (longer than usual days) and will end when Jesus (*pbuh*) will come and Muslims will kill all Jews. All people will convert into Islam. Peace will pervade the whole world.[11]

ISIS has a slick online magazine titled *Dabiq*, which is named after the town in Syria where one Muslim writing records Muhammad as predicting the final apocalyptic battle between Rome (Christians) and Muslims will take place. After the Muslims conquer Rome, the end times will begin with Muslims warring against the Antichrist.

The key to understanding ISIS lies in a small town in northern Syria, about 40 kilometers northeast of Aleppo. The name of the town, Dabiq, is synonymous with a concept in Islam under the same name that discusses a much-awaited battle between Islam and Christianity that will mark the end of the world. ISIS has made numerous claims that it wishes to quickly usher in the Armageddon, called *malahim* by the Muslims.[12]

As you can imagine, the end-time vision of ISIS is quite a powerful motivation and attractive recruiting tool for supporters and prospects. The message is simple: "The end of time is at hand, and if you want to be a true Muslim, on the right side of history, you had better join us. Come be part of the buildup to the final great battle." People flooding to the Middle East to join ISIS are seeking a role in the end-time drama. "In 2012, half of all Muslims in North Africa, the Middle East and S. Asia expected the imminent appearance of the Mahdi."[13]

THE PROOF IS IN THE FULFILLMENT

ISIS clearly believes they are a key player in their account of the apocalypse. They are paving the way for the final countdown to the end. The Bible, however, unveils a very different version of the end of days. According to Scripture, Jesus is coming back to rule over all. He will not be second fiddle to anyone.

What I find fascinating is that Islamic eschatology is an exact photographic negative of the one found in the Bible. Islam, which arose in the seventh-century AD, has taken many of the end-time predictions of Scripture and altered them to fit its viewpoint.

CHRISTIAN ESCHATOLOGY	ISLAMIC ESCHATOLOGY
The time before the return of Jesus is called the "Tribulation"	The upheavals of the apocalyptic last days are called "tribulations"
The return of Jesus ends the Tribulation, culminating the end of days	The return of Jesus heralds the last days

Jesus returns to Jerusalem to defeat the Antichrist	Jesus returns to Damascus to defeat Dajjal (the Antichrist figure in Islam)
Jesus delivers the Jewish people	Jesus leads Muslims to fight the Jews; He also shatters the crucifix and kills the swine
Jesus establishes a global kingdom of peace and prosperity on earth	The result of the return of Jesus and the Mahdi is a global Islamic caliphate

The ISIS (and overall Islamic) view of the end times presents a vastly different perspective of the end of days than that which appears in the Bible. So this is the next logical question: Which one is correct? Why should we believe what the Bible says any more than the Quran? Is there any objective way to know which of these competing eschatologies is true? Or if either one carries the ring of truth? Why should anyone believe the prophecies of the Bible as opposed to those in the Quran or any other alleged holy book?

Most people are probably not aware that more than one-fourth of the Bible was prophetic at the time it was written. The Bible is a book of prophecy. It contains about 1000 prophecies, about 500 of which have already been fulfilled down to the minutest detail. With this kind of proven track record—500 prophecies fulfilled with 100 percent accuracy—we can believe with confidence that the remaining 500 yet-to-be-fulfilled prophecies will also come to pass at the appointed time. Someone once commendably said, "We don't believe in prophecy because it's contained in the Bible, but we believe in the Bible because it contains prophecy." Prophecy is the most credible proof of the uniqueness and divine inspiration of the Bible. Its importance can hardly be overstated. About 110 prophecies were fulfilled in the life and ministry of Jesus alone. And 33 of them—very specific and distinct—were fulfilled during the final 24 hours of Jesus' life on earth.

Fulfilled prophecy validates the Bible and all the precious truths it contains. Think about it: If hundreds of biblical prophecies have been meticulously, accurately fulfilled, then it stands to reason that what the Bible has to say about other things—such as the nature and character of God, creation, the nature of man, salvation, and the existence of heaven and hell—are 100 percent accurate as well. It also demonstrates that the Bible's content is not man-made, but rather has its origins outside our own space-time continuum.[14]

The God of the Bible is so certain that only He can foretell the future that He issues a challenge to any would-be rivals to His place of supremacy in the universe. The basis of the challenge is that only the one true God can accurately predict the future. Read what He says about His unique ability to forecast the future:

> "Present your case," the LORD says. "Bring forward your strong arguments," the King of Jacob says. Let them bring forth and declare to us what is going to take place; as for the former events, declare what they were, that we may consider

them and know their outcome. Or announce to us what is coming; declare the things that are going to come afterward, that we may know that you are gods; indeed, do good or evil, that we may anxiously look about us and fear together. Behold, you are of no account, and your work amounts to nothing; he who chooses you is an abomination (Isaiah 41:21-24).

Islam makes no real claim that the Quran has foretold events that have come to pass. It lays out an elaborate end-time scenario, but provides no objective basis for believing that it will come to fruition. One must take it solely on faith. The Bible, on the other hand, gives overwhelming, credible evidence that its prophecies come true and therefore provides a solid basis for our confidence that its prognostications about the future will also come to pass. The Bible has a proven track record we can put to the test. This means its prophecies will be fulfilled just as the Bible promises. We can count on it. This means that in a strange, ironic twist the idea that ISIS is a harbinger of the coming of the end times might actually end up being true, but what actually happens will be far from the scenario its adherents have envisioned.

THE END OF ISIS OR THE END OF DAYS?

"Above all, ISIS seeks the fulfillment of prophecy, and even accepts it will come close to extinction in the process."[15] Defeating a rogue military force that believes it will come to extinction in the process of ushering in the end of days is not an easy undertaking. For them, death is victory. But the world seems to be slowly gathering the will to crush ISIS.

Some believe the air strikes that are pummeling ISIS are bringing its end within sight. Others say that only "boots on the ground" from the United States and other Western nations will finish the job. Could the United States and even NATO be roused to finally eradicate this scourge? Let's all hope so. The fall of ISIS would be welcome news to the entire civilized world, especially the victims of their gruesome atrocities in Iraq and Syria and in other places around the globe. Of course, no one knows for sure if, when, or how ISIS will meet its demise.

The Bible clearly states that God controls the nations and their leaders (Daniel 2:21; 4:17). God controls ISIS. It's important for us to remember that fundamental fact. We don't know all the reasons God has allowed ISIS to rise, but one reason could be that ISIS exists in some measure to reshape the Middle East in preparation for the final drama prophesied in the Bible.

Prophetically speaking, the survival of ISIS as a holder of territory is not significant. There are *no* biblical end-time prophecies *directly* related to ISIS. This is a critical point to remember. The importance of ISIS, from a prophetic standpoint, is the movements and reactions it has fostered—the reshaping it has influenced. There are at least three main ways ISIS has reshaped the Middle East and the surrounding nations.

First, ISIS has served as a potent catalyst to bring Russia into Syria—right on the northern border of Israel. Russian tanks, troops, and jet fighters are streaming into Syria under the guise of fighting ISIS. Russia is part of the Gog colossus that will invade Israel in the last days, according to Ezekiel 38. The presence of Russia on Israel's northern border is unprecedented and could be a run-up to the fulfillment of Ezekiel's ancient prophecy.

Second, ISIS has also given Iran motivation and a convenient justification to expand its influence in Iraq and station troops in Syria. Both Russia and Iran are now in Syria. They are poised on Israel's northern border. The Iranian-backed terror group Hezbollah has also joined the fight against rebel troops in Syria. The movement of Russian and Iranian forces into Syria could be a prophetic prelude to the formation of the Gog coalition and the invasion of Israel prophesied in Ezekiel 38–39. Both Russia and Iran are mentioned in Ezekiel 38. ISIS appears to be a precursor to the ultimate Islamic coalition against Israel—a Russian-Islamic alliance that will threaten the very survival of Israel in the end times.

Third, the chaos and carnage unleashed by ISIS may also serve to bring the Middle East nations to the peace table with Israel as predicted in the pages of Scripture (Daniel 9:27; Ezekiel 38:8,11). A region weary with war and bloodshed may finally be forced to forge a peace settlement. ISIS could be the compelling catalyst for a peace compact. We'll read more about this coming Middle East peace—albeit a fleeting, temporary one—in chapter 8.

It's safe to say that ISIS, while missing from the end-time biblical template, is a part of the overall complex or matrix of events that are pushing the world further down the road to Armageddon. They're part of the Middle East showdown that's fomenting and forcing the world to focus on that part of the world. However, the ultimate threat for Israel and the West, according to Scripture, is *not* ISIS, but rather, a Russian-Islamic alliance that will involve Iran as a key player. This threat *will* completely eclipse ISIS and play a key role in God's end-time drama. This end-time federation that could be looming just over the horizon is described in detail in Ezekiel 38–39, in a prophecy that describes what is commonly known as the Battle of Gog and Magog.

The Gog-Magog coalition may be coalescing before our eyes.

CHAPTER 4

The Ezekiel Prophecy

"Great events in history often gather momentum and power long before they are recognized by the experts and commentators on world affairs. Easily one of the most neglected but powerfully galvanizing forces shaping history in the world today is the prophecy of Gog and Magog from the 38th and 39th chapters of the book of Ezekiel."[1]

Jon Mark Ruthven,
The Prophecy That Is Shaping History

As you read these words, the Middle East is the number one hot spot in the world. ISIS is surviving and spreading into other nations. Russia has reasserted its dominance in the region. Israel and Iran are squaring off in a death struggle that points toward what the Bible predicts for the end times in the ancient prophecy found in Ezekiel 38–39. Much of what you read in today's headlines strikingly foreshadows this prophecy.

These two chapters, written almost 2600 years ago, describe a great coalition of nations, including Iran, that will invade the land of Israel when Israel is regathered and resting in her land in the latter years. It prophesies a great end-time conflagration commonly called the Battle of Gog and Magog. This will be the first of two great end-time wars. Before you read this chapter, it would be helpful to turn to appendix 4 and read Ezekiel 38–39 to familiarize yourself with these chapters.

To help us unpack this great prophecy and its meaning for today, I want to focus on four key points: the Allies, the Activities, the Annihilation, and the Aftermath.

THE ALLIES

Ezekiel 38 opens with a list of the nations that will constitute the invading force that will attack Israel in the end times:

> The word of the LORD came to me saying, "Son of man, set your face toward Gog of the land of Magog, the prince of Rosh, Meshech and Tubal, and prophesy against him and say, 'Thus says the Lord GOD, "Behold, I am against you, O Gog, prince of Rosh, Meshech and Tubal. I will turn you about and put hooks into your jaws, and I will bring you out, and all your army, horses and horsemen, all of them splendidly attired, a great company with buckler and shield, all of them wielding swords; Persia, Ethiopia and

Put with them, all of them with shield and helmet; Gomer with all its troops; Beth-togarmah
from the remote parts of the north with all its
troops—many peoples with you. Be prepared,
and prepare yourself, you and all your companies that are assembled about you, and be a
guard for them"'" (Ezekiel 38:1-7).

None of the place names in Ezekiel 38:1-7 exist on
any modern map. Ezekiel used ancient place names that
were familiar to the people of his day. While the names
of these geographical locations have changed many times
throughout history and may change again, the geographical territory remains the same. Regardless of what names
they may carry at the time of this invasion, it is these specific geographical areas that will be involved, as Thomas
Ice points out:

It appears that Ezekiel is using the names of peo
ples, primarily from the table of nations, and
where they lived at the time of the giving of this
prophecy in the sixth century B.C. Therefore, if
we are able to find out where these people and
places were in the sixth century B.C. then we
will be able to...figure out who would be their
modern antecedents today.[2]

Let's examine each of the ancient names to discover
the modern counterparts that will participate in this last-
days invasion of Israel.

Gog

The first name that appears is "Gog." This name appears eleven times in Ezekiel 38–39. From the context of Ezekiel, it's clear that Gog is the leader of this invasion and that Gog is an individual. He is directly addressed several times by God (38:14; 39:1) and is called a prince (38:2; 39:1). The word "Gog" may mean "height or mountain" and probably refers to the pride and arrogance of this leader. Others suggest that it comes from the Sumerian word *gug*, which means darkness. He will certainly bring darkness to the Middle East, acting "as a human eclipse, casting his shadow across the Middle East. It's an appropriate description of this coming evil leader."[3]

Many believe that Gog is the same person as the Antichrist. I don't agree with this view. I believe the Antichrist will lead the Western confederacy of the end times, while Gog will lead a Russian–Islamic coalition. Gog and the Antichrist will be enemies vying for power against one another.

Some have speculated that Russian leader Vladimir Putin could be Gog. He certainly is a "rising czar" in Russia. Of course, all such conjecture is needless, but as Joel Rosenberg has said, Putin is certainly "Gog-esque." Putin certainly provides a frightening portrait of the kind of leader who will someday emerge to lead this strike force against Israel.

Magog

The ancient Scythians inhabited the land of Magog.[4] The Scythians were fierce, northern nomadic tribes who inhabited territory that stretches today from Central Asia across the southern steppes of modern Russia. Modern Magog probably represents the former underbelly of the Soviet Union: Kazakhstan, Kirghizia, Uzbekistan, Turkmenistan, and Tajikistan. Russia could also be included in Magog as well as Afghanistan. All of these nations, other than Russia, are dominated by Islam, with a combined total population in excess of sixty million.

Rosh

Bible scholars have often identified Rosh in Ezekiel 38:2 with Russia. There is strong linguistic, historical evidence for making this connection.[5] Ezekiel predicts that the great Russian bear will rise in the last days to mount a furious invasion of Israel. The prophet Ezekiel predicted 2600 years ago that in the latter times Israel would be invaded by a people "from the distant north" or "remotest parts of the north" (38:6,15; 39:2). The nation to the distant or far north of Israel is Russia. Many mistakenly thought that when the Soviet Union was dissolved, the great Russian bear went into permanent hibernation. But the Russian bear today is a much more dangerous bear than ever before. The mighty Soviet Union has been dissolved; Russia has been left as a mother bear robbed of her cubs.

The fulfillment of God's prophecies concerning Russia seem more imminent than ever before. As we track the bear in the end times, we discover that her footprints lead right to the land of Israel. The preliminary setup for this invasion could be developing right before our eyes. Current events bear a remarkable correspondence to biblical prophecies. ISIS brought down a Russian airliner in late 2015, prompting Russia to move into Syria to take the fight to ISIS. Russia has troops, tanks, and airpower in Syria, not far from the northern border of Israel, and has a Mediterranean military port in Tartus, Syria. Russia is now closer than ever to Israel and shows no signs of leaving.

Think about it. If Israel is forced to take out the Iranian nuclear megacomplex, this will sow seeds of vitriolic hatred against Israel in Iran that could precipitate the Gog invasion in the near future. It could serve as the explosive catalyst for the nations in the Gog coalition to begin a plot for an all-out attack—a final payback against Israel. Such a strike could even be the "hooks in the jaws" that draw Russia into the fray. Russia has repeatedly warned Israel not to attack Iran.

General Jerry Boykin, a retired three-star general and former Undersecretary of Defense for Intelligence, has offered this perspective:

> If Israel were to strike Iran...you would see it accelerate the relationship between Russia and Iran. I think Russia would then come to the

aid of...the Iranians and I think you would see
that relationship solidify with increased military cooperation and military support, the sale
of additional military equipment and even military advice. And that sets the stage for ultimately what is described in Ezekiel 38 and 39.[6]

Things are clearly in a state of flux right now, but the
Bible is clear about where it's all headed and what will
ultimately transpire.

It's very possible that something like the scenario we
see unfolding today could be what God uses to pull a
reluctant Russia down into the land of Israel in the latter
years. Russia's geopolitical strategy to deepen its relation-
ships with Iran, Syria, and other Muslim nations could
very well be what will pull Russia into Israel in the end
times, as Ezekiel predicted.

Prophecy expert Thomas Ice envisions this kind of
future scenario.

I could see the Muslims coming to the Russians
and telling them that America has set a prece-
dent for an outside power coming into the Middle East to right a perceived wrong. (America
has done it again in recent years by going into
Afghanistan and Iraq.) On that basis, Russia
should help out her Muslim friends by leading
them in an overwhelming invasion of Israel in
order to solve the Middle East Conflict in favor

of the Islamic nations. Will this be the "hook in the jaw" of Gog? Only time will tell. But something is up in the Middle East and Russia appears to have her fingerprints all over things. We know that the Bible predicts just such an alignment and invasion to take place "in the latter years."[7]

Russia has a vital stake in Iran. The leadership of Russia, under Vladimir Putin, has carefully protected its interests in Iran and has consistently shielded Iran from any serious action by the U.N. Security Council:

> The pivotal consideration in Mr. Putin's efforts to re-establish his country's superpower status centers on Iran. Syria is a domino. Without its Syrian ally, Iran would be almost totally isolated and crucially weakened. That Moscow cannot allow. Why is Iran so central to Mr. Putin's global pretensions? Take a look at the Caspian Sea area map and the strategic equations come into relief. Iran acts as a southern bottleneck to the geography of Central Asia. It could offer the West access to the region's resources that would bypass Russia. If Iran reverted to pro-Western alignment, the huge reserves of oil and gas land-locked in Kazakhstan and Turkmenistan and the like could flow directly out to the world without a veto from Moscow...At stake here

is not merely the liberation of a vast landmass
from the Kremlin's yoke. The damage to Russian leverage would amount to a seismic shift in
the global balance of power equal to the collapse
of the Warsaw Pact. Russia's gas and oil leverage over Turkey, Ukraine and much of Europe
would evaporate.[8]

Putin cannot allow the mystique of Russian power to
deflate. Iran is the centerpiece of that image. Russian ties
with Iran have become very cozy in recent days. Massive
joint military exercises involving Iran, Russia, China, and
Syria point toward a coming war. Iran, Russia, China,
and Syria conducted a joint military exercise in the Middle East. Some 90,000 troops from the four countries
participated in land, air, and sea maneuvers off the Syrian coast, including air defense and missile units. In addition, about 400 warplanes and 1000 tanks took part in
the exercise. Egypt granted authorization for 12 Chinese
warships to sail through the Suez Canal. Russian atomic
submarines, warships, aircraft carriers, and Iranian bat-
tleships docked at Syrian ports. During the exercise, Syria
tested its air defense systems and coast-to-sea missiles.
Two Russian amphibious landing vessels landed at the
Russian base at the Syrian port of Tartus.[9] The current
close ties between Russia and Iran point toward the biblical prophecy in Ezekiel 38–39.

Meshech and Tubal

Meshech and Tubal are normally mentioned together in Scripture. They are listed two other times in Ezekiel (27:13; 32:26). The preferred identification is that Meshech and Tubal are the ancient Moschoi and Tibarenoi in Greek writings or Tabal and Musku in Assyrian inscriptions. The ancient locations are in present-day Turkey. This is best understood as a reference to modern Turkey, an Islamic country that is currently moving away from Israel and more and more toward its Islamic neighbors.

Persia

The ancient land of Persia became the modern nation of Iran in March 1935, and then the name was changed to the Islamic Republic of Iran in 1979. Iran's present population is about 80 million. Iran's regime is the world's number one sponsor of terror. Iran is making its bid for regional supremacy at the same time it is pursuing nuclear weapons.

Ethiopia (Cush)

The Hebrew word Cush in Ezekiel 38:5 is often translated "Ethiopia" in modern versions. Ancient Cush was called Kusu by the Assyrians and Babylonians, Kos or Kas by the Egyptians, and Nubia by the Greeks. Secular history locates Cush directly south of ancient

Egypt extending down past the modern city of Khartoum, which is the capital of modern Sudan. Thus, modern Sudan inhabits the ancient land of Cush. Sudan has recently divided. Northern Sudan is a hard-line Islamic nation that supported Iraq in the Gulf War and harbored Osama bin Laden from 1991 to 1996. It is not surprising that this part of Africa would be hostile to the West and could easily join in an attack on Israel.

Southern Sudan, which is mostly Christian, became Africa's fifty-fourth nation in July 2011. A referendum for independence in January 2011 was approved by an almost unanimous vote. The division of the nation into the Islamic north and mostly Christian south is another move that makes the fulfillment of the Ezekiel prophecy even more likely since the radical Islamic north will now be able to act on its own.

In light of the independence of southern Sudan, the Sudanese President Omar al Bashir stated that North Sudan will intensify its adherence to Sharia law:

> If the south Sudan secedes, we will change the constitution and at that time there will be no time to speak of diversity of culture and ethnicity. Sharia (Islamic law) and Islam will be the main source for the constitution, Islam the official religion and Arabic the official language.[10]

North Sudan is poised to take its place in the coming Gog alliance, just as Ezekiel predicted.

Libya (Put)

Ancient sources locate Put or Phut in North Africa. The Babylonian Chronicles, which are a series of tablets recording ancient Babylonian history, state that Put was the "distant" land to the west of Egypt, which would be modern-day Libya and could possibly include nations further west such as modern Algeria and Tunisia. The Septuagint, which was the Greek translation of the Old Testament, renders the word Put as Libues.

Modern Libya, an Islamic nation, suffered under the rule of Colonel Muammar al-Gadhafi from 1969 until the revolution in 2011. The madman was finally ousted, but the transition to another government has been rocky, to say the least.

In the wake of the revolution, a fragmented nation has emerged. Eastern Libya, where the country's oil fields are located, has threatened to seek a semiautonomous existence and eventually form a separate eastern state. ISIS is growing in Libya. ISIS is so committed to the caliphate that it is expanding in lawless Libya and getting closer and closer to the prized oil fields. Libya is the backup plan or fallback position for ISIS. If things don't work out in Iraq and Syria, ISIS believes the caliphate can simply move to Libya.

The central government of Libya has proved itself incapable of governing at all. Hope is dying:

> After the liberation from the rule of Gadhafi, Libyans dreamed their country of 6 million could become another Dubai—a state with a

small population, flush with petro-dollars, that is a magnet for investment. Now they worry that it is turning more into another Somalia, a nation with no effective government for more than 20 years.[11]

Libya appears headed for years of instability. Islamic jihadists, acting like vigilantes, have attacked shrines and monuments deemed un-Islamic. When the dust finally settles in Libya, the nation could find itself in the clutches of radical Islamic leaders who would gladly jump at the chance to be part of a coalition to invade Israel.

Gomer

Gomer refers to the ancient Cimmerians or Kimmerioi. Ancient history identifies biblical Gomer with the Akkadian Gi-mir-ra-a and the Armenian Gamir. Beginning in the eighth century BC, the Cimmerians occupied territory in Anatolia, which today is Turkey. Josephus noted that the Gomerites were identified with the Galatians, who inhabited what is now central Turkey.[12] Turkey is an Islamic nation with deepening ties with Russia. Turkey's natural allegiance is not to the European Union, but to her Muslim neighbors.

Beth-togarmah

Beth-togarmah means the "house of Togarmah." Togarmah is mentioned in Ezekiel 27:14 as a nation that traded horses and mules with ancient Tyre. Ancient

Togarmah was also known as Til-garamu (Assyrian) or Tegarma (Hittite) and its territory is in modern Turkey, which is north of Israel. Again, Turkey is identified as part of this group of nations that attack Israel.

THE END-TIME GOG COALITION	
Rosh (ancient Rashu, Rasapu, Ros, and Rus)	Russia
Magog (ancient Scythians)	Central Asia
Meshech (ancient Muschki and Musku)	Turkey
Tubal (ancient Tubalu)	Turkey
Persia	Iran
Ethiopia (Cush)	Sudan
Put or Phut	Libya
Gomer (ancient Cimmerians)	Turkey
Beth-togarmah (ancient Til-garamu or Tegarma)	Turkey

Many of these nations are either forming or strengthening their ties as these words are being written. This list of nations reads like the Who's Who of this week's newspaper. It's not too difficult to imagine these nations, all of whom are Islamic other than Russia, conspiring together to invade Israel in the near future, especially if Israel launches a preemptive strike against Iran.

Of course, the Bible never mentions Islam, since Islam was not founded until the seventh century AD, and the New Testament was completed in AD 95. However, isn't it interesting that all the nations in Ezekiel 38:1-7 that attack Israel in the end times are currently Islamic nations with the exception of Russia? And most of them are currently avowed enemies of Israel (Persia, Libya, and Sudan). There is nothing that these nations would love more than to invade Israel to wipe her off the face of the earth. Obviously, God knew this when Ezekiel penned his prophecy in about 570 BC, proving once again that the Bible is divine in origin.

The Protesters

Everything we see today suggests that Iran and the other nations in Ezekiel 39 are on a collision course with Israel and would gladly join with the Gog alliance of Ezekiel 38 when it comes together. However, we have to remember that there's also a sizable rift between Iran and the Sunni nations, such as Saudi Arabia and the Gulf States. The rift has become a full-blown rupture as Saudi Arabia has totally severed all ties with Iran. This corresponds to the picture presented in Ezekiel 38–39 as well.

When Russia, Central Asia, Iran, Turkey, North Sudan, and Libya (and possibly other nations) join together to assault Israel, a group of other nations sit on the sidelines, offering a lame protest to what's happening. This protest is recorded in Ezekiel 38:10-13.

> Thus says the Lord GOD, "It will come about on that day, that thoughts will come into your mind and you will devise an evil plan, and you will say, 'I will go up against the land of unwalled villages. I will go against those who are at rest, that live securely, all of them living without walls and having no bars or gates, to capture spoil and to seize plunder, to turn your hand against the waste places which are now inhabited, and against the people who are gathered from the nations, who have acquired cattle and goods, who live at the center of the world.' Sheba and Dedan and the merchants of Tarshish with all its villages will say to you, 'Have you come to capture spoil? Have you assembled your company to seize plunder, to carry away silver and gold, to take away cattle and goods, to capture great spoil?'"

The nations that lodge this objection are identified as "Sheba, Dedan and the merchants of Tarshish with all its villages." Sheba and Dedan are the nations we currently know as Saudi Arabia and the more moderate Gulf States. These nations, which are comprised of Sunni Muslims, are strongly opposed to Iran and its revolutionary posture and nuclear quest. It's no stretch to see them standing on the sidelines offering dissent to this future invasion. The actions of Sheba and Dedan in Ezekiel 38 fit what we see today.

The reference to "the merchants of Tarshish with all its villages" is not as easy to identify. Three ancient places were known as "Tarshish." First, there was a place with this name on the east coast of Africa, although the exact location is not known.[13] Second, another Tarshish was located in England. Third, a place known as Tartessus was in the present-day nation of Spain. The weight of authority seems to favor the third location. This was the view of the Hebrew scholar Heinrich Friedrich Wilhelm Gesenius.[14] In biblical times, Tarshish was a wealthy, flourishing Phoenician colony located in what is now Spain, and it exported silver, iron, tin, and lead (Jeremiah 10:9; Ezekiel 27:12,25).

According to the New American Standard Bible (NASB), Ezekiel also refers to "the merchants of Tarshish with all its villages" (38:13). Compare the translation offered by the New International Version (NIV): "the merchants of Tarshish and all her villages." But the translation presented by the King James Version (KJV) is probably the best: "Tarshish, with all the young lions thereof." Young lions are often used in Scripture to refer to powerful, energetic rulers. Therefore, the young lions who join with Tarshish to verbally oppose Gog's invasion could be strong military and political leaders who act in concert with Tarshish.

Another possibility is that the phrase "all the young

lions"—or "all its villages," as the NASB has it—refers to the nations that have come out of or originated from Tarshish.[15] If this is correct, the question again is, Where was Tarshish in Ezekiel's day? Apparently it was in the farthest western regions of the known world, which would be somewhere in what is now Spain.

The prophet Jonah was commanded by God to go preach to Nineveh (about 500 miles northeast of Israel). But Jonah headed as far in the opposite direction as he could go, which was to Tarshish (Jonah 1:1-3). Spain, of course, is in modern Europe. More specifically, it is in western Europe. Tarshish, or modern Spain, may be used by Ezekiel to refer to the nations of western Europe who will join the moderate Arab states in denouncing this invasion. Tarshish is often associated with the west in Scripture: "The western kings of Tarshish and other distant lands will bring him tribute" (Psalm 72:10 NLT).

The young lions of Tarshish could be a reference to the colonies that emerged from Europe, including the United States. If this is true, then the young lions of Tarshish describe the United States in the last days joining in with her European and Saudi-Gulf State allies to lodge a formal protest against the Russian-Islamic aggressors. If Tarshish was in England, then the "young lions thereof" could refer to "the United States, Canada, Australia, New Zealand, and other present-day western democracies" that came from England.[16] If so, this would be a clear biblical reference to the role of America in the end times. However, this lone reference seems too tenuous for me to fully get on board with the perspective that America is in view anywhere in Bible prophecy.

Nevertheless, whether you take these young lions to refer to the United States or to the Western powers of the last days, the scenario that is presented in Ezekiel 38 fits the present world political situation to a *T*. Russia continues to flex its muscle in the Middle East by forging alliances with Iran and Arab nations. The Islamic nations of ancient Magog (Central Asia) are developing and deepening ties with Iran, Russia, and Turkey. The Middle Eastern Muslim nations' hatred for Israel continues to fester and boil. It's not too difficult to imagine the nations mentioned in Ezekiel 38:1-7 coming together under Russian leadership to mount a furious attack against Israel. It's also not difficult to imagine the Western powers of the last days objecting to the attack.

The Near Enemies

Ezekiel 38 lists what is often described as the "far enemies" of Israel. If you look on a map, you will see that the nations listed are the farthest enemies of Israel in every direction: Russia to the north, Iran to the east, Sudan to the south, and Libya to the west. This raises an important question: What will happen to the near enemies of Israel, such as Jordan, Egypt, Gaza, Syria, and Lebanon? They aren't mentioned in Ezekiel 38. Does the Bible say anything about the fate of these nations?

Some commentators have answered this question by

saying that Psalm 83, which lists the main near enemies
of Israel, refers to a separate war that will precede the war
in Ezekiel 38–39 and will dispose of Israel's near enemies.
They believe that the destruction of Israel's near enemies,
which they often call the Psalm 83 War, will pave the
way for the rest and security that Israel will enjoy (Ezekiel
38:8,11). While this scenario could be correct, I prefer to
see Psalm 83 as similar to Psalm 2 and not as a separate
end-time war.

Psalm 2 highlights the ages-long hatred and conspir-
acy of the nations against the Lord and His anointed One,
the Messiah. The similarities with Psalm 83 are apparent.
Nations are conspiring against the Lord and the Davidic
King.

The Lord scoffs at them and predicts a time when
(1) they will be destroyed, (2) His King will rule the earth,
and (3) people will submit to Him. This looks ahead
to the messianic kingdom or 1000-year reign of Christ,
which brings the end times to a head. The main difference between these two passages is that Psalm 2 does not
specifically enumerate the nations, but Psalm 83 lists ten
specific enemies.

Nevertheless, the point is the same. The enemies of
God and His anointed King will one day be destroyed
and will submit to Him. People don't look for some separate "Psalm 2 War." Instead, they see it as a general
prophecy that the Lord's enemies will be destroyed in the
end times. I believe that's the same thing that's going on
in Psalm 83.

We have to remember that the Psalms were written long before the prophets began to write and give specific prophecies concerning the nations. The prophets are where we look to find specific prophecies concerning the nations and end-time events. The Psalms certainly do contain messianic prophecies, but I'm not aware of other specific, detailed prophecies in the Psalms concerning the Gentile nations in the end times.

I believe that constructing a separate end-time war out of Psalm 83 is reading too much into a text that is simply saying that Israel has been and always will be surrounded by enemies and that someday the Lord will finally deal with them. In Psalm 83, God is bolstering and encouraging the nation and its king at the very beginning of the Davidic reign, promising that He will ultimately prevail over His enemies and will protect His people from extinction.

So what will happen to Israel's near enemies? It could be that the Bible simply doesn't tell us about their immediate fate. Or they could be included in the Battle of Gog and Magog. The mention of the far circle of nations around Israel could include the near nations as well. After all, the final words of Ezekiel 38:6 are "many peoples with you." This could be a catch-all to include other nations not specifically mentioned in Ezekiel 38:6, and some of the near enemies of Israel could be included in this description.

Islam and Ezekiel 38–39

Ironically, Islam has its own version of the Battle of
Gog and Magog, called the War of Yajuj and Majuj, but
it's very different from that which is described in the biblical account. In two places, the Quran specifically mentions "Gog and Magog" (Yajuj and Majuj) by name
(18:96; 21:96). Islamic eschatology teaches that there are
ten major signs that signal the approach of the end and
the day of resurrection. There are various opinions about
the order of these signs, but in at least one list, Gog and
Magog is the number four sign.

According to Islamic teaching, Gog and Magog are
two groups of Turks that were spreading corruption
through the earth during the time of Abraham. Finally,
to keep them in check, they were enclosed behind a great
barrier. They tried in vain to climb over it and have been
trying to dig under the wall for centuries, but they will
not be able to get out until Allah decrees that they can
be released. Then the barrier will collapse, and Gog and
Magog will pour out in all directions, rushing into the
land of Israel to attack the Muslims there. When Jesus
prays against Gog and Magog, Allah will wipe them out
by means of some kind of disease or plague that he will
send upon them. The disease is described as either infec-
tious, lethal boils, or an affliction that eats the flesh from
their bones.

If that sounds familiar, it should. It was evidently
taken by Muhammad straight from Ezekiel 38, with a
few convenient changes made to fit his own ends. Ezekiel

38:22 specifically says that God will destroy the invaders with pestilence and with blood. Therefore, while Muslims believe in the prophecy of Gog and Magog, they appear to be totally ignorant of the fact that all the nations that will be destroyed by God in Ezekiel 38 are Muslim nations today, with the exception of Russia. One of their ten great signs of the end will actually be fulfilled by them when they attack Israel in the last days.

THE ACTIVITY

Ezekiel says that these nations led by Russia, and with Iran as a key participant, will come against Israel "after many days" at a time when the people of Israel are living in peace ("at rest," "securely") and prosperity (38:8-12). The timing of this invasion is the most debated issue. It has been placed at about every point in time in the latter years. Many excellent prophecy teachers believe the battle of Gog and Magog could occur before the rapture happens, or at least before the Tribulation period begins. Proponents of this view believe the Gog-Magog War could happen at any time, which certainly adds a sense of urgency to what's transpiring today. While this view is certainly possible, Ezekiel says the invasion occurs in the "last days" or "latter years" for Israel, which I believe begin with the Tribulation period. For this reason, I don't believe it can happen before that time.

Others equate this invasion with the Campaign of Armageddon that will transpire at the end of the

Tribulation period. The main support for this view is that both events are attended by a great bird supper feeding on the carnage (Ezekiel 39:4-5,17-20; Revelation 19:17-18). Although this similarity is noteworthy, it's not unusual that two different wars could each include a feasting by the birds. The primary problem with this view is that Israel will not be at rest at the conclusion of the Tribulation. Israel will have endured three-and-a-half years of persecution by the Antichrist by that time, so the peace prerequisite for the invasion will not be present.

All things considered, I believe this invasion will transpire during the first half of the coming seven-year Tribulation, when Israel will be living under her peace treaty with Antichrist. Ezekiel repeatedly emphasizes that when this invasion occurs, Israel will be back in the land "living securely" (38:8,11,14) and "at rest" (38:11). Although some would argue that Israel today is "living securely" and "at rest," I believe that's quite a stretch when one looks at the current situation in Israel.

The language in Ezekiel 38 seems to fit best with the conditions we can expect during the first half of the coming seven-year Tribulation. However, one should avoid dogmatism concerning the timing of this invasion, and here's why: Excellent prophecy teachers disagree about this aspect of the prophecy. All we can say for sure about it is that it's future. No event in the past even comes close to fulfilling the events described in Ezekiel 38–39.

What we know for sure is that this invasion will occur sometime in the future. When the massive foray into Israel takes place, Russia and her Islamic allies will descend upon the nation of Israel "like a storm" and "will be like a cloud covering the land" (38:9). From the text of Ezekiel and parallel Old Testament passages, there are four main reasons why Russia and her allies will invade Israel.

1. *To cash in on the wealth of Israel (Ezekiel 38:11-12).* The exact nature of this wealth is never specifically stated, but some people speculate that it could involve the vast oil and gas reserves that are currently being discovered and tapped in Israel. A gargantuan deposit of natural gas was discovered off Israel's Mediterranean coast in December 2010, and an even larger area of shale oil has been found near Jerusalem. More finds have come in the Golan Heights. It's believed these discoveries will turn Israel into a net exporter of oil and gas. The Arabs in the Middle East no longer have a monopoly on energy.

2. *To control the Middle East.* While this is not specifically stated in the text, one can assume that this would be part of any invasion of this magnitude.

3. *To crush Israel.* The Islamic nations mentioned in Scripture hate Israel and would love nothing more than to "come like a storm" and "like a

cloud covering the land." This invasion will look like the long-awaited fulfillment of the Muslim dream to drive the Jews into the sea.

4. *To challenge the authority of Antichrist.* If I'm correct about the timing of this invasion during the first half of the Tribulation, Israel will be under her peace treaty with Antichrist at the time of this attack.

Therefore, the attack against Israel (the Battle of Gog and Magog) will represent a direct challenge by Russia and its Islamic allies to Antichrist and the West. After the armies of Ezekiel 38 are destroyed by God, Antichrist will break his covenant with Israel and invade the land himself (Daniel 11:41-44). The destruction of the Russian-Islamic army will leave a gaping power vacuum that the Antichrist will also quickly move to fill, eventually establishing his one-world government and economy at the midpoint of the seven-year Tribulation. He will rule the world for the final three-and-a-half years of the age.

THE ANNIHILATION OF THE INVADERS

When these nations invade the land of Israel, it will look like the biggest military mismatch in history. It will make the invasions of Israel in 1967 and 1973 by the Arab nations pale in comparison. When this last-days strike force sweeps into the land, it will look like Israel is finished forever. But God will be in control of the entire situation. He will mount up in His fury to destroy these godless invaders: "'It will come about on that day, when Gog invades the land of Israel,' declares the Lord GOD, 'that My fury will mount up in My anger. In My zeal and in My blazing wrath...'" (Ezekiel 38:18-19).

God will come to rescue His helpless people and will use these means to destroy Russia and her allies:

1. He will send a great earthquake (38:19-20).

2. There will be infighting among the troops of the various nations (38:21). In the chaotic aftermath of the powerful earthquake, the armies of each of the nations represented will turn against each other. This will be the largest case of death by friendly fire in human history.

3. The invaders will also experience dreadful disease (38:22).

4. God will send torrential rain, hailstones, fire, and burning sulfur (38:22).

The famous Six-Day War occurred in Israel in June 1967. This will be the One-Day War (or even the One-Hour War), when God supernaturally destroys this Russian-Islamic horde.

THE AFTERMATH OF THE WAR

Four key events will unfold in the aftermath of this invasion.

1. *The arrival of the birds and the beasts (Ezekiel 39:4-5,17-20; cf. Revelation 19:17-18).* The carnage that results from this slaughter will provide a great feast for the birds of the air and the beasts of the field. God refers to the carnage as "My sacrifice" and "My table" to which He invites the birds and the beasts as His guests.

2. *The seven-month burying of the dead (Ezekiel 39:11-12,14-16).* Clean-up squads will be assembled to go through the land. They will set up markers wherever they see a human bone. When the gravediggers come behind them, they will see the markers and take the remains to the Valley of Gog's Hordes for burial. The cleansing will be so extensive that a town will be established in the valley at the gravesites to aid those who are cleansing the land. The name of the town will be Hamonah ("horde").

3. *The seven-year burning of the weapons (Ezekiel 39:9-10).* Since the Battle of Gog and Magog occurs during the first half of the Tribulation, the Israelites will continue to burn the weapons from this battle on into the millennial kingdom for three-and-a-half years.

4. *The blessing of salvation (Ezekiel 39:25-29).* In the midst of His wrath and fury, God will also pour out His grace and mercy. God will use the awesome display of His power against the invading armies to bring many to salvation among both Jews and Gentiles.

God makes it clear that He will have the last word:

> I will bring you against my land as everyone watches, and my holiness will be displayed by what happens to you, Gog. Then all the nations will know that I am the LORD...I will make myself known to all the nations of the world. Then they will know that I am the LORD...Then they will know that I am the LORD. In this way, I will make known my holy name among my people of Israel. I will not let anyone bring shame on it. And all the nations, too, will know that I am the LORD, the Holy One of Israel...In this way, I will demonstrate my glory to the nations....And from that time on the people of Israel will know that I am the LORD their God (Ezekiel 38:16,23; 39:6-7,21-22 NLT).

Many of those who turn to the true God as a result of this demonstration of His power will undoubtedly be among the vast group of the redeemed in Revelation 7:9-14.

CONCLUSION

Over and over again in Ezekiel 38–39, God makes it clear that He is in charge. If there's one thing we learn above all else from this passage, it's that God is in control. He says to these future invaders, "I will turn you about and put hooks into your jaws, and I will bring you out" (Ezekiel 38:4). God pictures these invading nations as a huge crocodile that He drags out of the water.

In Ezekiel 38–39, seven times we read the same words: "Thus says the Lord GOD" (38:3,10,14,17; 39:1,17,25). Another eight times we see this refrain: "declares the Lord GOD" (38:18,21; 39:5,8,10,13,20,29). Obviously, God doesn't want us to miss the point—this is His Word. The prediction in Ezekiel 38–39 comes directly from Him. He is the author of the script.

In other places, God further emphasizes that He is sovereignly at work in human affairs:

- "You will be summoned" (38:8).

- "I will bring you against My land" (38:16).

- "I will turn you around, drive you on, take you up...and bring you against the mountains of Israel" (39:2).

Obviously, God is not violating the will of these invaders by bringing them into Israel. They want to come. They "devise an evil plan," and God holds them responsible for it (38:10). Nothing in this statement is meant in any way to lessen the human responsibility for these events. The point is that ultimately, God is in control. He is the director. He is the one who will make sure the stage is perfectly set for His great prophetic production.

God has scripted many events and participants to play certain roles in His prophetic production. And as we have seen, one of the major events that God has scripted for the end times is the Battle of Gog and Magog. It is the first major military campaign of the end times.

The rise of militant Islam has shocked and surprised most people. But amazingly, some 2600 years ago, God predicted through the prophet Ezekiel the exact scenario that we see developing before our eyes every day on the evening news.

Ezekiel 36–39 is "history written beforehand." Ezekiel 36–37 describes the regathering of the Jewish people to the land of Israel in the end times. Then this regathering will be followed by an all-out invasion of Israel by a massive assault force, according to Ezekiel 38–39. On May 14, 1948, Israel became a nation against all odds, preparing the way for the first part of Ezekiel's prophecy to be fulfilled. As we look around today, it appears that the stage is being set for the rest of his prophecy to come to pass exactly as God predicted.

All the nations in Ezekiel 38 are identifiable countries with the will and desire to eliminate Israel. Many of these nations are forming alliances with one another. ISIS

is helping set the stage. The crisis between Iran and Israel
has reached a boiling point that could spill over to the
entire Middle East, toppling dominoes that will further
pave the way for this predicted war. The world is yearning for peace in the Middle East, and this peace will bring
about the rest and security that must exist for this invasion to occur.

In all of this, Iran is a key place to watch. We see
events in Iran and places all over the Middle East
splashed across the television screen and news headlines
every day, and they are like runway lights beginning to
light up as the coming of Christ approaches.

CHAPTER 5

Showdown in the Middle East: Iran and Israel

*"God willing, there will be no such thing
us a Zionist regime in 25 years. Until then,
struggling, heroic and jihadi morale will leave
no moment of serenity for Zionists."*[1]

Ayatollah Ali Khamenei

*"The Middle East could continue to deteriorate into
superpower proxy client states, all with a destabilized
nuclear arms component; or the region could seek
genuine peace. Iran's recent missile test and its now
documented underground missile bases assure movement
toward an apocalyptical nuclear scenario."*[2]

Steven Horowitz

The Middle East is at war. Iran and Israel are at war.
Israel and Iran have been at war—a shadow war—
since the founding of the Islamic Republic of Iran in

1979. That date marked the beginning of Iran as the world's number one supporter of terror, and it was the start of its direct opposition to the state of Israel. The rhetoric from Iran has been ratcheted up since the mullah regime took the reins of power.

Many believe that the trouble between Iran and Israel began with the election of former Iranian President Mahmoud Ahmadinejad, who denied the holocaust and regularly expressed his desire for Israel to be wiped off the map. But he was simply echoing what the Ayatollah Khomeini had said repeatedly decades earlier.

The six world powers (United States, Britain, China, France, Germany, and Russia) tirelessly tried diplomacy for more than a decade to curb Iran's nuclear program, and round after round of sanctions have slowly tightened like a noose since 2006. Iran worked the "talk and build" strategy to perfection. They delayed, stalled, and played for time. They teased the West with overtures of a possible diplomatic solution while the underground nuclear facilities were expanded and reinforced and while the centrifuges continued to spin. Iran's diplomatic dance bought precious time for it to advance its nuclear ambitions, but the point of no return finally arrived in July 2015. After years of grinding, grueling negotiations, world powers finally reached a "landmark" deal with Iran on limiting Iranian nuclear activity in return for the lifting of international economic sanctions. The deal reportedly gives U.N. nuclear inspectors extensive but not automatic access to Iranian sites.[3]

One provision of the deal allows Iranian access to $150 billion in previously frozen assets—money that can shore up Iran's shaky economy and fund terrorist activities.

From Friend to Foe

In light of the current state of affairs, it's difficult to imagine that until 1978 and the Islamic revolution, Iran was actually friendly toward Israel. Reaching much further back, in about 538 BC, the Persian king Cyrus the Great was a generous benefactor of the Jewish people, allowing them to return to their ancient homeland to rebuild the temple. (For more about Cyrus and the biblical prophecies dealing with ancient Persia, see appendix 1.) Iran's ancient predecessor, the mighty Persian Empire, was a benevolent friend of the Jewish people and was used by God to bless them. It's tragic that the current leadership of Iran, which traces its heritage back to Cyrus, now denies the Jewish people's claim to the land of Israel and wants to wipe them off the face of the earth.

Fast-forwarding to the twentieth century, Iran was still a friend of Israel after the establishment of the modern state of Israel in 1948—even when the Arab nations surrounding Israel mounted a campaign to drive the Jews into the sea. The Iranians, who are Persians, not Arabs, and who speak Farsi, not Arabic, adopted a much more positive view toward the Jewish state, as Yaakov Katz and Yoaz Hendel observe:

On the surface, it is not obvious that Israel and Iran are enemies. The countries do not share a border, but they do share a rich history as two of the only non-Arab countries in the greater Middle East. Diplomatic ties between Israel and Iran were initiated immediately after the establishment of the Jewish state in 1948 under Israel's first prime minister, David Ben-Gurion, and lasted until Ayatollah Ruhollah Khomeini came to power in 1979, turning Iran from one of Israel's closest friends into its fiercest enemy. Israel's undeclared war with Iran began in the 1980s, when Iran founded Hezbollah; it has grown to even greater proportions since the Second Lebanon War in 2006, as have Hamas and Islamic Jihad in the Gaza Strip, also with Iranian assistance.[4]

Until 1978, Iran was actually a trusted ally of Israel. But that all changed suddenly and dramatically when the Iranian revolution broke loose and the Shah of Iran was deposed. The theocracy that replaced the Shah was under the control of Ayatollah Khomeini, who turned the nation against the United States (the great Satan) and Israel (the little Satan). Iran's shadow war with Israel began in 1979, and it joined the chorus of Arab nations who deny the right of Israel to exist. As long as Israel is in the land, they will never cease in their drive to destroy her. Over the decades since, the posture of Iran toward the United States

and Israel has hardened and become much more dangerous, especially with the outing of Iran's nuclear program in
2003.

Consider the following chart:

KEY DATES IN IRAN'S HISTORY	
550 BC	Cyrus the Great rose to power over the Medo-Persian Empire.
539 BC	Medo-Persians overthrew the city of Babylon, just as Daniel predicted in Daniel 5.
538 BC	King Cyrus allowed the Jewish people to return to Israel, ending the 70-year Babylonian captivity. Isn't it ironic that the same nation God used to allow the Jewish people to return to their national homeland over 2500 years ago is now denying their right to that land and wants to wipe them off the map?
480–473 BC	Esther married King Xerxes, and the story in the book of Esther unfolded in Persia.
444 BC	King Artaxerxes allowed Nehemiah to return to Israel to rebuild the walls of Jerusalem and restore the city.
334–331 BC	Persia was overwhelmed by Alexander the Great in a series of crushing defeats, as predicted in Daniel 8.
March 21, 1935	The name Persia was changed to Iran.
1978–79	Ayatollah Ruhollah Khomeini led the Islamic Revolution in Iran.

April 1, 1979	The name of Iran was changed to Islamic Republic of Iran.
November 4, 1979	A U.S. embassy in Tehran was seized, and 52 hostages were taken. The crisis lasted 444 days.
1982	Iran founded Hezbollah in Lebanon.
1987	Iran acquired nuclear centrifuge technology from Dr. Abdul Qadeer Khan, a renegade Pakistani engineer.
January 1995	Russia signed an $800 million nuclear plant deal with Iran to complete the nuclear plant at Bushehr.
November 2004	Iran agreed to suspend uranium enrichment.
August 2005	Mahmoud Ahmadinejad won the Iranian presidential election in June and was installed as the president of Iran in August.
January 9, 2006	Iran rebuffed European diplomatic efforts and resumed uranium production at its plant in Natanz, claiming that its only intention was to make reactor fuel to generate electricity.
March 29, 2006	The UN Security Council unanimously approved a statement demanding Iran suspend uranium enrichment.
April 9, 2006	Iran officially announced that it had begun enriching uranium.
June 2009	Mahmoud Ahmadinejad is reelected as the president of Iran.
2009–2012	Rounds of sanctions and talks are conducted.

2012	Talk of an Israeli strike against Iran escalates amid renewed negotiations and strengthened sanctions.
2015	A nuclear deal, that Iran must shrink and open up its nuclear program to inspection, is reached between Iran and the six world powers.
2016	The Iran nuclear deal is slated to go into effect.

QUEST FOR THE BOMB

Iran's nuclear quest began in the late 1980s, when Abdul Qadeer Khan, a renegade Pakistani nuclear engineer, sold nuclear enrichment technology to Iran. Since that time, Iran has been carrying out a clandestine nuclear weapons program, although its pride as a possessor of nuclear power is on full display on the Iranian currency (the rial). The Iranian 50,000-rial banknote has the nuclear symbol on its reverse side. It's like saying, "In Nukes We Trust." What does this tell us about Iran? The nuclear pursuit is now so deeply ingrained in the Iranian psyche that it's an integral part of their national pride. To them, to surrender this right would be the ultimate humiliation.

Iran has agreed to the nuclear deal, but at the same time its leader regularly chants "Death to America," and has said that Israel won't exist in twenty-five years. Within just a few months of agreeing to the nuclear deal, Iran twice tested ballistic missiles capable of carrying a nuclear payload. While doing a few things to go through the motions, Iran shows every sign that the agreement is meaningless and that it will covertly carry on its nuclear weapons program.

One specific indication of Iran's defiance is that Iranian president Hassan Rouhani has accelerated production of missiles. According to senior Iranian commander General Hossein Salami, Iran's Revolutionary Guards have so many missiles they don't know where to hide them all. He said, "We lack enough space in our stockpiles to house our missiles. Hundreds of long tunnels are full of missiles ready to fly to protect your integrity, independence and freedom."[5] These precision-guided Emad missiles can carry a nuclear warhead and can reach Israel.

Iran knows that once sanctions are removed and it receives its frozen assets and access to world markets, it will take a long time to ever reinstate the sanctions, if they can even be reinstated at all. Iran also knows that any violations of the deal will take months to investigate and any decisions issued by the powers that put the deal together will come forth at a painstakingly slow pace.

One thing is certain: Iran will work the system at every turn.

The Syria Connection

While Iran and ISIS are archenemies, ISIS has provided Iran with an open invitation into Iraq and Syria. Under the guise of fighting ISIS, Iran has spread its

influence into Iraq and shipped troops into Syria, one
of its key surrogates. Iran is a strong backer of Bashir al-
Assad, the Syrian president, and has used the ISIS crisis
in Syria as a justification to move troops there. Top Iranian military commander Soleimani was spotted in Syria
in October 2015 rallying Iranian officers and Hezbollah
terrorist fighters. Hezbollah, the Iranian-backed terror
group in Lebanon, has also moved into Syria to help Iran
and Russia shore up the Assad regime. Iran could never
have dreamed of such an opportunity to get its troops sta-
tioned so easily in Syria. ISIS has provided that window.

Iran and the Bear

Iranian troops have been joined by Russian tanks,
troops, and airpower. Russia is working hand in hand
with Iran in Syria, right on the northern border of Israel.
In fact, Russia and Iran are working together on several
fronts. When sanctions are removed from Iran as part of
the nuclear deal, Russia plans to build two nuclear reac-
tors in Iran and sell its long-range S-300 surface-to-air
missile system to Iran.

Could these movements just north of Israel be part of
the prelude to prophetic fulfillment?

How Long Will Israel Wait?

Authors Yaakov Katz and Yoaz Hendel set the scene
for what we might see unfold in the near future as tension
mounts over Iran's nuclear pursuits:

The briefing room will be packed when the prime minister takes his position at the podium and asks everyone to sit down. As the young pilots stare up at their nation's leader, the prime minister will gaze right into their eyes, searching for one more confirmation that he has made the right decision.

While clearly nervous, the pilots are ready. They have been prepared for this day for the past few years, some of them from the beginning of their Israel Defense Force service. The prime minister does not have much to say.

"This is a historic day for our small nation," he will announce. "Some seventy years ago Nazi Germany tried to destroy our people, but we survived and succeeded in establishing the State of Israel. It is now up to you to ensure that we will continue to survive and live here."

Then the rabbi for the Israeli Air Force will stand up at the podium, and all of the pilots will cover their heads. Together they will say the Traveler's Prayer, a short plea to God written at the time of the Talmud, to ask that they make it to their destination and return safely.

At once, the pilots stand and salute the prime minister, the defense minister, and IAF commander. Minutes later, they climb inside their aircraft and begin lining them up along the runway.

The prime minister had actually made up his mind to attack Iran several months earlier but had waited, hoping to coordinate the operation

with the White House. While the president
tried to persuade Israel to back down and even
threatened to cut military aid, the Israeli leader
explained that he was not asking for permission. Instead, the prime minister asserted, he
was doing what allies do and informing the
president of his government's decision ahead
of time. The Israeli cabinet had spoken: Iran's
nuclear program had to be stopped.[6]

One thing is clear. If Israel feels compelled to launch
a preemptive strike against Iran's nuclear sites, things will
never be the same. Not for Israel. Not for the Middle
East. Not for the world. The attack will trigger a cascade
of events that could bring strong retaliation from Iran
and its proxies Syria, Hezbollah, and Hamas, all of whom
may pound Israel with rockets and missiles. Israel could
find itself fighting fierce onslaughts on the northern front,
the southern front, and the home front. Such a war could
spark a wider regional conflict, with Iran attacking American forces in the Persian Gulf and Saudi oil fields. The
question of what America will do is unclear. Some fear
that an Israeli preemptive assault could even start World
War III.

Israel has vowed that it will take out the Iranian
nuclear facilities if Iran fails to stand down in its nuclear
aspirations. Israeli General Daniel Halutz was asked back
on March 7, 2006, "How far would Israel go to stop
Iran's nuclear program?" He calmly responded, "2000
kilometers."[7] That's the distance from Israel to Iran.

What General Halutz said in 2006 has not changed. To the contrary, Israeli resolve has hardened. Israel will go to any lengths to interrupt the Iranian nuclear machine. Despite assurances from Iran, the Iranian nuclear program is still running. International Atomic Energy Agency (IAEA) officials have already expressed their doubts concerning full Iranian compliance.

Iran and Israel are already at war. Open conflict appears inevitable. Jeffrey Goldberg observes, "Netanyahu isn't bluffing—he is in fact counting down to the day when he will authorize a strike against a half-dozen or more Iranian nuclear sites."[8] Israel believes that it has the capacity to cause enough damage to set Iran's nuclear program back by three to five years.[9] *The New York Times* has envisioned an Israeli surgical strike by 100 planes.[10] Note also this article by D.B. Grady:

> No sane person would wish for a unilateral Israeli strike on Iranian nuclear facilities—but nor would a sane person wish for a nuclear Iran...But if intelligence suggested an impending, existential threat to Israel, it's easy to imagine F-15I fighter jets planting GBU-28 bunker-busters in Iranian nuclear sites from the Caspian Sea to the Persian Gulf. And if that happens, the real question becomes, what next?[11]

That's the question everyone is asking. What's next? Will there be an Iranian counterstrike? What will it look like? How aggressive and far-reaching will it be? What will Hezbollah and Hamas do? Will the United States be drawn into the fray? Could it trigger a larger regional war? Or even World War III? No one knows the nature and extent of the immediate fallout. There will undoubtedly be many twists and turns. But is it possible that these events are part of a larger drama scripted long ago?

ISRAEL AND THE UNITED STATES IN THE CROSSHAIRS

The mullah regime in Iran, according to Israeli prime minister Benjamin Netanyahu, poses an "existential threat" to Jewish people and their homeland. Iranian leaders continue to spew out venom against Israel that openly unmasks their evil intentions. Iran's supreme leader Ayatollah Ali Khamenei has referred to Israel as a "cancerous tumor that should be cut and will be cut."[12] Several Iranian defectors have made it clear that Khamenei is directly involved in the nuclear program. He makes the final decisions. Scientists who have defected from Iran have given differing measures of the state of Iran's nuclear development, but "they were all clear about Iran's true intentions, however: the Islamic Republic was developing the bomb so it could one day attack Israel."[13]

Alireza Forghani, a strategy specialist and staunch supporter of Supreme Leader Ayatollah Ali Khamenei, has released a detailed military plan to annihilate Israel, which he claims can be accomplished in less than nine minutes using Iranian missiles. He maintains that

"Tehran is capable of annihilating Israel within less than nine minutes using its arsenal of missiles and by deploying operational combat units throughout the world."[14] He says that Iran will hit targets inside Israel, including nuclear facilities, air force bases, and civilian infrastructure. Ayatollah Khamenei has warned of a "lightning response" to any preemptive attack by Israel. He said, "Should they take any wrong step, any inappropriate move, it will fall on their heads like lightning."[15]

But Israel is not alone as the focus of Iranian malice. For the Iranian regime, the United States is part of its plan for annihilation. Ayatollah Khamenei stated, "In light of the realization of the divine promise by almighty God, the Zionists and the Great Satan [America] will soon be defeated."[16] Some Israeli officials claim that Iran is working to develop a long-range missile capable of reaching the United States. Americans believe the threat posed by Iran is great. A CNN poll found that fear of Iran in the United States "has surpassed fear of the Soviet Union during one of the Cold War's most dangerous years."[17] The poll revealed that 81 percent of Americans believe Iran is a "very serious" or "moderately serious" threat, with 48 percent calling it "very serious."[18] Eighty-four percent of Americans believe Iran is developing nuclear weapons, and 71 percent believe they already have the bomb.[19]

It Will Be Much Harder This Time

The Israeli success in destroying the nuclear facilities in Iraq and Syria will be much more difficult, if not impossible, to replicate. Iran is a nation of about 80 million people inhabiting 1.65 million square kilometers and the nuclear targets in Iran are 1000 miles from Israel. It is the eighteenth largest country in the world in size, and the seventeenth largest in population.

Also, Iran's nuclear program is not concentrated in one location or even one facility. It's spread out across seven places.

Iran's Seven Key Nuclear Facilities

Bushehr Nuclear Power Plant

This Russian-built nuclear reactor began producing electricity in 2010.

Arak Heavy Water Reactor

This facility is able to produce weapons-grade plutonium. The Iran nuclear deal requires Iran to disable the heavy water reactor.

Natanz Enrichment Facility

Iran has two main uranium enrichment facilities: Natanz and Fordo. Iran's oldest and largest one at Natanz is the main enrichment center. Surrounded by antiaircraft batteries, it's located partly underground, and it can hold up to 50,000 centrifuges, but only 5000 can work under the nuclear agreement.

Isfahan Nuclear Technology Center

Built in 2006, it converts yellowcake to uranium hexafluoride.

Tehran Nuclear Research Center

This center is made up of labs where nuclear research is conducted.

Bandar Abbas Uranium Production Plant

This plant processes uranium ore.

Fordo Uranium Enrichment Plant

Buried 300 feet underneath a mountain next to a military complex, this site was kept secret until it was identified by Western intelligence agencies in September 2009. Iran finally had to acknowledge the existence of the facility at that time. The facility, which resides inside a hardened tunnel, is protected by air defense missiles and the Iranian Revolutionary Guard. It can hold up to 3000 centrifuges.

A DAUNTING TASK

Taking out Iran's nuclear facilities or even stunting their growth for a few years would be a daunting task. "The Natanz complex consists of two large halls, roughly 300,000 square feet each, dug somewhere between eight and twenty-three feet below ground and covered with several layers of concrete and metal. The walls of each hall are estimated to be two feet thick."[20]

At Iran's Fordo site near Iran's holy city of Qom, centrifuges have been churning out uranium enriched to more than 20 percent, which "can be turned into fissile warhead material faster and with less work."[21] This level of enrichment is not necessary for industrial use. Under the nuclear deal, most of Iran's nuclear stockpile of enriched uranium (more than 20,000 pounds) has been loaded on ships and sent to Russia for safekeeping. Of course, Russia could return the material to Iran at any time or allow amounts to be smuggled there in the future. Iranian uranium in Russian hands for safekeeping is hardly a comfort to Israel.

The heavily fortified Fordo facility is buried 300 feet under a mountain, which means that inflicting significant damage will be difficult. Ehud Barak has stated that the facility is "immune to standard bombs."[22] In spite of the daunting challenges, Israel will be forced to strike and inflict whatever damage possible unless there is some drastic change.

The choice for Israel is quickly narrowing to two options: Either they carry out the bombing, or they suffer the bomb. And both Israel and the United States have said forcefully and repeatedly that they will not allow Iran to get the bomb. The nuclear deal does not require Iran to dismantle its nuclear infrastructure, which only delays the inevitable. The ten-year "sunset clause" in the agreement delays Iran from getting its hands on the bomb but guarantees it will happen at some point. Israel has little confidence in the inspection protocol of Iranian nuclear facilities, pointing out past covert operations by Iran and the fact that inspections totally failed in the case of North Korea.

So, barring some unforeseen, unimaginable walk-back by Iran and verifiable compliance with the nuclear deal, the only option for Israel at some point in the future is to bomb Iran's nuclear facilities. Michael Oren, Israeli Ambassador to the United States, framed the issue succinctly: "America, a big country, has a big window, looks out that window and sees the Middle East far away; Israel, a small country with a very small window, we look out that window and we see Iran in our backyard."[23] That's the issue. A nuclear Iran is not an option for Israel. In the wake of the nuclear deal going into effect, Israel has issued stern warnings. "Israel has issued a stark, public warning to its allies with a clear argument: Current proposals guarantee the perpetuation of a crisis, backing Israel into a corner from which military force against Iran provides the only logical exit."[24]

If Iran goes nuclear, it could transfer a nuclear device to one of its terrorist proxies to be detonated in Israel or the United States. A nuclear Iran would also trigger a nuclear arms race in the world's most volatile region. As Israeli defense minister Ehud Barak says, "The moment Iran goes nuclear, other countries in the region will feel compelled to do the same. The Saudi Arabians have told the Americans as much, and one can think of both Turkey and Egypt in this context, not to mention the danger that weapons-grade materials will leak out to terror groups." Henry Kissinger also sounds the alarm about Iran's drive to the nuclear finish line: "If Iran is allowed to produce nuclear weapons, the genie will be out of the bottle, and the whole world will be in grave danger."[25] Imagine terrorist organizations in the Middle East getting their hands on a nuclear weapon or even radioactive material to make a "dirty bomb." A nuclear-armed Iran will also push the most militant factions within Hezbollah and other Iranian surrogates to step up their aggression and take greater risks.[26]

THE VOICE OF THE PROPHETS

Of course, all the recent developments with Israel and Iran present formidable economic, political, and military challenges for the United States, Israel, and other Western nations. A great deal of diplomatic capital has been expended. There are no easy solutions. Confrontation looms.

But could the rise of Iran and its stance toward Israel have even greater significance? Could events we are witnessing today be preparing the way for the fulfillment of Bible prophecy? Only God knows for sure, but many signs point in that direction. As alarming as current events are in the Middle East, they shouldn't be surprising in light of the end-time prophecies of the Bible.

The biblical prophecy in Ezekiel 38–39, written about 2600 years ago, tells us that a great horde of nations will invade Israel in the last days while Israel is at rest in her own land. The leader of this invasion will apparently be Russia, and one of the main allies in this confederation of nations, according to Ezekiel 38:5, is Persia—the modern nation of Iran. Russia has risen to world prominence in the last century, and it has experienced a great resurgence in the last decade. Iran is now world public enemy number one and an avowed anti-Semitic state, which has pledged to wipe Israel off the map.

I want to be clear that I don't believe the current crisis in Iran and the Middle East is the direct fulfillment of any biblical prophecy. However, it is an ominous development that strikingly foreshadows what the Bible predicts. It is a significant signpost that I believe points toward the fulfillment of the great prophecy of Ezekiel 38–39. In the surging events in the Middle East, we can hear the pounding of prophetic hoofbeats.

An Israeli strike against Iran's nuclear facilities would undoubtedly unleash a vicious backlash. Dominoes would begin to fall. No one knows for sure how they would fall, or how many would fall, but we know some would fall. We also know that some consequences would develop immediately, while others might slowly smolder. But one thing is clear: The Iranian mullahs already harbor a devilish hatred for the United States and Israel. Just think how they would respond if Israel struck their nuclear program. Any military action by the United States or Israel (or both) against Iran would undoubtedly plant seeds of vengeful animosity in Iran that could later erupt in the fulfillment of the biblical prophecy in Ezekiel 38–39. We may be witnessing the stage-setting for this incredible prophecy right now! The pieces of Ezekiel's prophetic puzzle seem to be coming together, with the end-time stage being set right before our eyes.

IN THE THEATER OF WORLD EVENTS

The setting of the world stage for end-time events can be graphically illustrated by picturing a theater where preparations are being made for a production. Suppose a drama critic who happens to be an expert on Shakespeare were to enter that theater one evening, not knowing what Shakespearean play is to be presented. Before the curtain goes up, he is taken behind the scenes.

On stage is a castle with fortifications looking out over a wooded countryside. At once he knows that the play is not *Othello*, which is set in Venice, nor *Julius Caesar*, which begins with a street scene in Rome. He knows that it is not *Macbeth*, for even though a castle scene does take place in *Macbeth*, the play opens not with the castle but with witches gathered around their cauldron. Finally, our drama critic notices two soldiers with shields bearing the arms of the king of Denmark. He sees an actor and actress who are dressed up as a king and a queen, and one actor who is supposed to be a ghost. Now no one has to tell the critic what he will see, for he knows it will be *Hamlet*.

In the same way today, God's people sit in the theater of world events awaiting the curtain call of God's apocalyptic drama. We don't know when the play will begin, but like the drama critic, we know much more about it than most. Many people attempt to look ahead into the future and see only a huge curtain. For them, the future is veiled—they have no idea of what God plans to do. And they can't see behind the curtain where Act One is being set. But as believers, with the Bible's help, we have the opportunity to see the setting-up that will take place behind the scenes. While it is true that we don't know the moment when the play will begin, we do know some information about the play itself—the main characters and events—and we can sense that we're approaching the opening scene as we see the actors starting to take their proper places on the great world stage.[27]

The Jewish people are back in their ancient homeland after being scattered to 70 countries for almost 2000 years. They are surrounded by a sea of enemies, just as Scripture predicted. Iran has risen to prominence as both the dominant military power in the Middle East and the world's largest state sponsor of terror. At the same time, the Russian bear has roared out of hibernation to reassert its influence and lend its support to the Iranian regime. The world economy is teetering on the brink of recession or even worse. People everywhere are crying out for peace in the Middle East.

Behind all of this looms the ancient prophecy of Ezekiel 38–39, which predicts that Iran (ancient Persia) will be a key player in the end times and that Iran will join a confederacy of other nations to attack Israel. What we see happening appears to point toward the fulfillment of this great prophecy.

Beyond all of this, Iran is ruled by a mullah regime in the grip of an apocalyptic madness that drives it. This ideology will undoubtedly play an integral role in what will happen in the days ahead and on into the end times.

CHAPTER 6

Show Me the Mahdi

"Who can think that Iran poses no threat to world peace? History tells us that when madmen call for genocide, they usually mean it."[1]

Mortimer Zuckerman, *U.S. News & World Report*

In addition to Iran's hatred for Israel and its nuclear quest, as if those two factors weren't bad enough, Iran holds to an apocalyptic ideology, which is the belief that it can hasten the end of the world and bring about the global rule of Islam. Since the Islamic revolution in 1979 and the formation of the Islamic Republic of Iran, the Iranian mullah regime has led the nation in a deepening death spiral. Joel Rosenberg, an expert in Bible prophecy and geopolitics, graphically describes Iran's leadership as "an apocalyptic, genocidal death cult."[2] Those are strong words, but sadly, they are true. Iran's leadership is under the spell of a form of Shiite Islam known as "Twelver Shiism."

The majority of Muslims in the world today—about 85 percent—are Sunnis. Though Shiites are fewer in number overall, they are the dominant part of the population in Iran, Iraq, and Bahrain. The difference between Shiites and Sunnis stems from a controversy over who is qualified to lead the religion. Understanding the particular strain of Shiite Islam that dominates Iran opens a frightening window into the thinking of its mullah regime and at least some of the motivation behind their actions.

HASTENING THE END

According to Shiite Islam, an imam is a spiritual leader who is allegedly a bloodline relative of the prophet Muhammad. There is a prophecy in Islam about the coming of the Twelfth Imam—Imam Muhammad Abul Qasim. It's believed by the Twelver sect that in AD 874, when the Twelfth Imam was five years old, he disappeared in the cave of the great mosque of Samarra without leaving any descendants. He was hidden by God. It's also taught that the Twelfth Imam was still active and communicated through messengers until AD 941. At that point the sect believes all communication and contact with this world was cut off. They call the Twelfth Imam the Hidden Imam and the *Mahdi* (Arabic for "rightly guided one"). Since the tenth century, they have been waiting for the Mahdi to emerge to lead them to victory and subjugate the world. This brings us to a major difference between the views of ISIS and Iran concerning the end of days: They both believe in the Mahdi as a key end-time figure, but ISIS believes the Mahdi is coming, while Iran believes he is already here but is in hiding.

According to Islamic teaching, the Mahdi will make his appearance near the end of the world:

> The mullahs leading Iran's Islamic regime believe in the messianic return of the 12th and last Islamic messiah, Imam Mahdi. According to Shiite belief, Mahdi will reappear at the time of Armageddon, and his coming will be triggered by the destruction of Israel. In a recent statement, Grand Ayatollah Jafar Sobhani, a religious authority and a top Iranian "Twelver Shia"—one who believes in the 12th Imam—addressed the future world described in the Quran. "The Quran is the proof that the world will be controlled and managed by the forces of truth and that there will be one government ruling everyone throughout the world," he explained. The Quran promises—twice—the worldwide rule of Islam and its victory over all other religions, Sobhani said, and this will only happen when the last descendant of Muhammad, Imam Mahdi, returns and takes the rule of Islam across the world. Ayatollah Khamenei referred to this prophecy in a recent speech. "In light of the realization of the divine promise by almighty God," he said, "the Zionists and the Great Satan [America] will soon be defeated. Allah's promise will be delivered, and Islam will be victorious."[3]

This end-time view, or eschatology, teaches that when the Hidden Imam returns, he will rule the earth for seven years, bringing about the final judgment and end of the world. The mention of a seven-year rule for the Mahdi is interesting to students of Bible prophecy because the Bible predicts that the final Antichrist or false messiah will hold sway over the earth for seven years, ruling the entire world for the final half of the seven-year period. Could the Islamic expectation of a messiah who will rule for seven years set them up to initially accept such a leader, one who will make a seven-year peace treaty, according to Daniel 9:27?

In any event, Iran's politics cannot be divorced from its fundamental religious views about the Hidden Imam.

To demonstrate how deep the anti-Semitism runs among Iran's leadership, Iran's vice president used the lectern of an international antidrug conference in New York in June 2012 to deliver a baldly anti-Semitic speech, blaming Judaism's holy book for teaching how to suck blood from people. He also stated that Jews control the world drug trade and were responsible for the Bolshevik Revolution in Russia in 1917.[4]

Behind all the anti-Semitism and bravado lies the mystical Islamic theology that sees current events in the Middle East preparing the way for the coming of the Mahdi, Islam's messianic figure. Several years ago, when Mahmoud Ahmadinejad was still the president of Iran, Anton La Guardia made this chilling observation about Ahmadinejad's "Apocalypse Now" theology:

> After a cataclysmic confrontation with evil and darkness, the Mahdi will lead the world to an era of universal peace...Indeed, the Hidden Imam is expected to return in the company of Jesus. Mr. Ahmadinejad appears to believe that these events are close at hand and that ordinary mortals can influence the divine timetable. The prospect of such a man obtaining nuclear weapons is worrying. The unspoken question is this: is Mr. Ahmadinejad now tempting a clash with the West because he feels safe in the belief of the imminent return of the Hidden Imam? Worse, might he be trying to provoke chaos in the hope of hastening his reappearance?[5]

While Ahmadinejad is no longer president, this sentiment is still in place among Iran's leaders. Iran's mullahs believe that the Mahdi controls events in Iran and around the world and that things are shaping up quickly for his coming. War with Israel and the United States and the ensuing chaos is a kind of "welcome mat" for the Mahdi.

They believe an end-time war will sweep the Mahdi to power. Iran's participation in a regional or even global conflict could be viewed as a self-fulfilling prophecy.

FAST FACTS ABOUT THE MAHDI

- The Mahdi won't come in an odd year (Islamic calendar).

- He will appear in Mecca.

- He will travel from Mecca to Kufa (Iraq).

- He will be 40 years old at the time of his emergence.

- He will remove all injustice, bringing universal prosperity.

- Jesus will return with him and be his deputy.

- The Mahdi will wear a ring that belonged to King Solomon.

- He will carry the wooden staff of Moses.

- He will conquer his enemies, who will be led by the one-eyed Antichrist (Dajjal).

- He will rule for 7 years (some say 9 or 19 years).

ISLAMIC BELIEFS ABOUT THE MAHDI

- Islam's primary awaited savior

- Descendant of Muhammad

- Caliph and Imam of Muslims worldwide

- Unparalleled political, military, and religious world leader

- Revealed after period of great turmoil and suffering on earth

- Establishes justice throughout the world

- Leads a revolution to establish a new world order
- Will go to war against all nations who oppose him
- Makes a seven-year peace treaty with a Jew of priestly lineage
- Conquers Israel for Islam and leads final battle against the Jews
- Rules for seven years, centered in Jerusalem
- Causes Islam to be the only religion on earth
- Discovers biblical manuscripts that convince Jews to convert
- Brings the Ark of the Covenant from the Sea of Galilee to Jerusalem
- Has power from Allah over wind, rain, and crops
- Will possess and distribute great wealth
- Face will shine like a star and he will be loved by all

Joel Rosenberg summarizes the ideology that drives Iran:

> American leaders need to better understand Shia eschatology. The Twelfth Imam was a real flesh-and-blood person who, like the eleven Shia leaders who went before him, was an Arab male, a direct descendant of the founder of Islam, and was thought to have been divinely chosen to be the spiritual guide and ultimate

human authority of the Muslim people. His actual name was Muhammad Ibn Hasan Ibn Ali, and it is generally believed by Shias that he was born in Samarra, Iraq, in AD 868. At a very young age, however, Ali vanished from society. Some say...the Mahdi's mother placed him in the well to prevent evil rulers from capturing him and killing him, and that little Ali subsequently became supernaturally invisible. This is where the term "Hidden Imam" is derived, as Shias believe that Ali is not dead but has simply been hidden from the sight of mankind— Shias refer to this as "occultation"—until the End of Days, when Allah will reveal him once again. Shias believe the Mahdi will return in the last days to establish righteousness, justice, and peace. When he comes, they say, the Mahdi will bring Jesus with him. Jesus will be a Muslim and will serve as his deputy, not as King of kings and Lord of lords as the Bible teaches, and he will force non-Muslims to choose between following the Mahdi or death. By most accounts, Shia scholars believe the Mahdi will first appear in Mecca and conquer the Middle East, then establish the headquarters of his global Islamic government—or caliphate—in Iraq. But there is not universal agreement. Some believe he will emerge from the well at the Jamkaran Mosque in Iran and then travel to Mecca and Iraq. Some say that he will conquer Jerusalem before establishing his caliphate in Iraq. Others believe Jerusalem must be conquered as a prerequisite to his return. None of this is actually written in the Koran, and Sunnis reject this eschatology. But one thing that is fairly well agreed upon among devout "Twelvers" is that the Mahdi will end apostasy and purify corruption within Islam. He is expected to conquer the Arabian Peninsula, Jordan, Syria, "Palestine," Egypt and North Africa, and eventually the entire world. During this time, he and Jesus will kill between 60 and 80 percent of the world's population, specifically those who refuse to convert to Islam.[6]

Current events in the Middle East are interpreted by Iran as a sign of the Mahdi's soon coming and an open door for them to expand their influence. Iran is seizing what it believes is an opportunity for it to foster its own purposes.

Is the Mahdi the Biblical Antichrist?

Any discussion of the Islamic Mahdi requires a consideration of his possible relationship to the biblical Antichrist. There are a growing number of prophecy teachers and authors who are claiming that the coming Antichrist or world ruler will be a Muslim. That he will be the manifestation of the Islamic messiah (Mahdi) possibly from a nation like Iran or even a group like ISIS. With the meteoric rise of Islam on the international scene, the growing adherence to this view is not surprising. Those who hold this view often reject the idea of a reunited Roman

Empire centered in Europe as the dominant force in the end times. For them, world power is dominated by a Muslim caliphate and ruled over by the Islamic messiah.

This identification is based on several points. First, they often cite the basic fact that Islam is the fastest-growing religion in the world, including in the United States, Canada, and Europe, and that in a very short time it will pass Christianity as the world's largest religion. From this they argue that it simply makes sense that the world's final military, political, spiritual leader will be from this majority religion. My response to this point is that we must be careful not to interpret prophecy in light of current events, but rather view current events through the lens of Scripture. Looking at biblical prophecy through the headlines is often called "newspaper exegesis" and can lead to unwarranted sensationalism.

Second, adherents of this view sometimes note that the vast majority of the nations that are listed as key end-time players in the Bible are currently Islamic nations—geographical locations such as Syria, Jordan, Egypt, Sudan, Libya, Lebanon, Turkey, Iran, etc. Since these are the key end-time nations, they argue that it makes the most sense if the coming world ruler is a Muslim from one of these nations. They also usually hold that Gog in Ezekiel 38–39, the leader of an end-time invasion against Israel, is the same person as the Antichrist. We will address that issue later. Although it is true that the staging ground for the end times is the nation of Israel, the

Bible also mentions a final form of the Roman Empire in Daniel 2 and 7. Ezekiel 38 refers to "Rosh," which many believe is modern Russia. Revelation 16:12 also identifies a great military confederation from east of the Euphrates called the "kings from the east" that will pour into the Middle East in the end times. So the idea that all the nations mentioned in end-time prophecy are Islamic nations is an overstatement.

Third, proponents of this view point to the many similarities between the Muslim Mahdi or messiah and the biblical Antichrist. Lists of similarities are cited: Both will be world rulers, both will be spiritual world leaders, both will make seven-year treaties, and both ride on a white horse.[7] These similarities are cited as proof that these two end-time figures are the same. But is it not possible that the reason for the similarities is that Muhammad got so much of his information from the Bible stories he heard from Jews and Christians?

Fourth, the Bible says that the Antichrist will be a terrible persecutor of the Jewish people. Those who hold to the Islamic Antichrist position note that the Mahdi will launch a targeted campaign against Jews and Christians, will attack Israel, and will establish the seat of his authority on the Temple Mount just as the Bible predicts in 2 Thessalonians 2:4. Because the Temple Mount is under Muslim control, they believe this is consistent with an Islamic Antichrist figure. However, it seems very unlikely to me that an Islamic Mahdi would sit in a rebuilt Jewish temple to declare himself god. Any Muslim worth his salt would destroy the Jewish temple—not sit in it.

Fifth, some highlight the fact that the Antichrist will use beheading as a form of execution against those who reject his rule (Revelation 20:4). They hasten to point out that this is a favorite means of execution among followers of Islam, epitomized by the savagery of ISIS. While this is true, beheading was the chief method of execution in the French Revolution, and whatever his background, the Antichrist could revive this form of execution because it's simple, swift, and would add to the sense of terror for those who are thinking about rejecting his rule. He could simply adopt the practice from ISIS, seeing the terror it arouses.

Sixth, Daniel 7:25 says of the coming Antichrist that "he will speak out against the Most High and wear down the saints of the Highest One, and he will intend to make alterations in times and in law; and they will be given into his hand for a time, times, and half a time." Joel Richardson views this as a key clue that the Antichrist will be the Muslim Mahdi. He says,

> This is actually quite a big hint into the person of the Antichrist. For by his actions, we see a hint of his origin. It is said that he will desire to change two things: times and laws. Now we have already seen that the Mahdi will change the law by instituting the Islamic Shariah law

all over the earth, but we have not seen any evidence in Islamic apocalyptic literature of him changing the "times." The simple question however is, who else other than a Muslim would desire to change the "times and laws"?...Islam, however, does have both its own laws and its own calendar, both of which it would desire to impose onto the entire world. The Islamic calendar is based on the career of Muhammad.[8]

It is obviously true that Muslims have a calendar that is different from the one in the Western world, and it is true that if Muslims ever could gain control of the world, they would enforce the observance of their calendar. However, the Antichrist is going to change the calendar regardless of who he is or what his religious background may be because the calendar followed by most of the world counts time from the birth of Jesus. The Antichrist's changing of times and laws will be his attempt to remove any vestige of Christianity from the world. It is not necessary for the Antichrist to be the Islamic Mahdi in order to fulfill this prophecy.[9]

The only passage of Scripture I know of that gives insight into the religious background of the Antichrist is found in Daniel 11:36-39. Describing the final world ruler as "the king [who does] as he pleases," Daniel said,

He will exalt and magnify himself above every other god...He will show no regard for the gods

of his fathers or for the desire of women, nor
will he show regard for any other god; for he will
magnify himself above them all. But instead he
will honor a god of fortresses, a god whom his
fathers did not know; he will honor him with
gold, silver, costly stones and treasures. He will
take action against the strongest of fortresses
with the help of a foreign god.

While I would agree that there are some interesting
parallels between the biblical Antichrist and the Islamic
Mahdi, for me, this passage precludes the Islamic Antichrist view. Daniel said that the Antichrist will exalt himself above every god and will honor a god that his fathers
did not know. The Antichrist could be someone who was
a Muslim at some point in his life, but this passage indi-
cates that by the time he comes to power, he must have
rejected Allah and turned to another god, the god of fortresses or military might and ultimately himself. So if he
is a Muslim at some point in his life, which is possible,
this passage makes clear that when he comes to power he
will have turned his back on all religions and established
himself as god.

Second Thessalonians 2:4 makes it clear that the Antichrist will take his seat in the temple of God, which is a
reference to a rebuilt or third Jewish temple in Jerusalem,
and will declare that he is god. No practicing Muslim
could ever do this. Certainly the Islamic Mahdi couldn't.
This would violate the central tenet of Islam that there is

one God, who is Allah. If the Mahdi were to declare himself god, then he would no longer be a follower of Islam. Joel Richardson, who supports the Muslim Antichrist view, admits the problem this argument raises for his view but provides this response:

> We need to understand that the Antichrist will not demand worship until well after the fact that he has been universally acknowledged and accepted by the Islamic world as the Mahdi. The Imams, mullahs, sheiks, and the Ayatollahs, all of the world Islamic leadership, will have given their allegiance to the Mahdi. To deny him after this point would be the ultimate shame for Islam. It would come at a time when Islam will universally be experiencing its greatest rush of vindication and fulfillment. In the midst of all this incredible elation, to suddenly declare and acknowledge that an absolute evil charlatan had deceived the entire Islamic world would be unthinkable. Once the deception has taken place, it will be impossible to undo. The hook will have been set.[10]

This answer overlooks the fact that for the Antichrist to declare himself to be god would be the ultimate act of brazen blasphemy. No self-respecting Muslim could ever accept this. To believe that Islamic leaders would still follow someone who claimed to be the Islamic Mahdi and then later declared himself to be God is naïve. If the modern rise of radical Islam teaches us anything it's that their leaders are ardent zealots unwilling to compromise on lesser points of religious practice, let alone the major tenet of their faith.

Another problem with the Islamic Antichrist view is that the final world leader will leap on the world scene as a great peacemaker (1 Thessalonians 5:3). In Revelation 6:1-2 he emerges at the beginning of the Tribulation as a false Christ riding a white horse counterfeiting the coming of Jesus Christ at the end of the Tribulation as a conquering hero (Revelation 19:11-21). As Charles Dyer and Mark Tobey observe,

> A weary world will welcome this leader and Antichrist as someone who will finally resolve its many problems and bring peace. The apostle Paul describes the start of this tribulation period as a time when people will be saying "Peace and safety!" (1 Thessalonians 5:3). When the Antichrist arrives, he will offer Israel and the world global peace. Many will trust him because of his promise of safety and security. It's hard to imagine the rest of the world viewing the arrival of an Islamic Antichrist, especially of the brand of ISIS, with any sense of peace and safety. Our reaction to the rise of ISIS has been just the opposite. Neither Israel nor the West find

comfort in Islamic conquerors accompanied by
such barbaric strategies and impulses.[11]

I agree with this assessment and believe it applies equally
to any Islamic leader, not just someone from ISIS.

A final related issue that precludes the Islamic Antichrist or Mahdi Antichrist view is that this final world
ruler will make a seven-year treaty or covenant with Israel
that brings peace, a treaty he will break at the midpoint
of the Tribulation (Daniel 9:27). He will have the trust
of Israel. The question is, How could the Jewish people
ever put their national security in the hands of an Islamic
ruler? How could they trust a devout follower of Islam?
The events of the past seventy years have given Israel no
reason to trust any Muslim leader with the security of
their nation. Israel would never trust a devout follower
of Islam with an issue of this gravity for their survival. It's
totally counterintuitive.

For these reasons, I don't hold to the Islamic/Mahdi
Antichrist view. I believe the Bible teaches that the final
Antichrist will be a God-hating, Christ-rejecting mega-
lomaniac who will despise every religion and every god
other than himself and his ultimate master, Satan.

What Will Iran Do?

Iran's apocalyptic beliefs about the Mahdi and the
notion that they can hasten the events of the end of

days heightens the fears surrounding Iran's pursuit of nuclear weapons. A nation with such beliefs should never be allowed to possess the bomb. They cannot be counted on to act rationally and with the normal sense of self-preservation.

All of this raises a critical question: What will Iran do? Do the mullahs really believe the final chapter has begun and that they can help bring it to fruition? Will their apocalyptic ideology drive them to seize the opportunity to unleash a regional or even global conflict that they believe will bring the Mahdi, or do they have the survival instinct that will lead them to hold their cards until some later time? Time will tell. But ultimately, according to the ancient prophecies of Ezekiel, Iran will join with a coalition of allies to attack Israel at the end of days. We may be witnessing the beginning of the buildup for this end-time war.

AMERICAN ASSISTANCE OR ABSENCE?

The great *X* factor in the future of the Middle East is the United States. What will America do? Will the United States make the commitment to destroy ISIS? Will the United States hold Iran to the conditions of the nuclear deal? Will America come to Israel's aid when they are threatened, or choose to sit this one out? No one knows for sure. There are so many variables in play that no one can say for sure. Israel might not even give the United States advance notice if it decides to strike Iran's nuclear facilities. But one thing is certain: The United States will play some role in the conflict if things begin to spiral out of control. This raises an often-asked and often-debated issue: What is America's role in the end times? Does the Bible provide any clues about the future of America?

CHAPTER 7

What Will Happen to America?

"America is not mentioned anywhere in the Bible, implying that it would be crippled or taken out of the picture in some way."[1]

Glenn Beck

People everywhere are wondering where the Middle East crisis is headed. All eyes are on ISIS, Iran, and Israel. This book is primarily about these players and how current events involving them point toward biblical prophecy.

But one of the most-asked questions today in Bible prophecy is, Where is the United States in the end times? America is the key player in the world today and figures heavily in the ongoing events in the Middle East. America is the lone superpower in the world. Will this continue into the end times? What is America's role in all this?

One thing is certain: Americans are war-weary as the conflict in Iraq has ended and the more-than-a-decade-long war in Afghanistan has ground to an uncertain end. We all wonder if this nation will be dragged into another Middle East conflict. Will the United States lead the attack against Iran's nukes, will it aid Israel in some way, or will it remain on the sidelines? Will Iran target U.S. interests if Israel strikes? Will ISIS continue to survive and spread, or be stopped? What does the Bible say, if anything, about America's future? I've been asked this last question so many times that I wrote a book to address all the issues related to America in Bible prophecy. The book is titled *The Late Great United States: What Bible Prophecy Reveals about America's Last Days*. The thesis of the book is that America is not mentioned in the Bible, either directly or indirectly, and that this silence is significant. America is not "Babylon the great" (Revelation 17–18), the unnamed nation (Isaiah 18), the ten lost tribes of Israel, or the "young lions" of Tarshish (Ezekiel 38:13 KJV). America is missing in action in the end-time prophecies of the Bible.

The Scriptures reveal that the major superpower in the end times, at least by the midpoint of the Tribulation, will be a reunited Roman Empire (Revelation 13:4). This dominance by the nations in a revived Roman Empire can only be explained in light of America's decline. Prophecy scholar John Walvoord sees no major end-time role for America:

Although conclusions concerning the role of America in prophecy in the end time are necessarily tentative, the Scriptural evidence is sufficient to conclude that America in that day will not be a major power and apparently does not figure largely in either the political, economic, or religious aspects of the world.[2]

Charles Ryrie agrees:

The Bible has made crystal clear the destiny of many nations. Babylon, Persia, Greece, Rome, Egypt, Russia, and Israel...But not so with the United States...The Bible's silence concerning the future of the United States might well mean that she will play no prominent role in the end-time drama. A nation does not have to be named in order to be identified in Bible prophecy. When Ezekiel described the future Russian invasion he used the phrase "remote parts of the north" (38:15). Surely some prophet would have predicted something about those countries or peoples in the remote parts of the West if God had intended a major end-time role for them in the Western Hemisphere. The fact is that no one did...Instead, we are led to conclude that the United States will be neutralized, subordinated, or wiped out, thus having little or no part in the political and military affairs of the end time.[3]

To be sure, I don't want to see the United States decline. I love this country, but it seems unlikely to me that the United States will play a key role in the end times. But what could reduce America to a subordinate role? What kind of event could bring America to its knees? While we cannot speak with certainty at this point—since the Bible doesn't tell us—we can make some educated guesses. Several plausible scenarios fit the current world situation. They could occur alone, or in a fatal combination. Over the last few years, we have witnessed major developments on three fronts that threaten the continued role of America as the world's superpower. These three fronts are moral (internal decay), military (external threat of nuclear terror), and monetary (economic hazard of a diminishing role for America and the dollar). Let's briefly consider each of these mounting perils.

CAUSES FOR THE DECLINE OF AMERICA

Moral Meltdown

For America, the news on the moral front is not good. We are rapidly approaching a disastrous 50-percent out-of-wedlock birthrate. The dreaded scourge of abortion continues unabated, with the total now over 50 million since 1973. Pornography is an industry of more than $12 billion, and it is infecting our young people every day. According to the Centers for Disease Control, 26 percent of American girls between the ages of 14 and 19 have at least one sexually transmitted disease.[4] Added to all this, the homosexual movement continues to propel its agenda forward, tragically affirming America's deepening slide into the death spiral of judgment described in Romans 1:26-32. This passage describes how God's wrath is revealed against nations by giving people over or abandoning them to the ravaging consequences of their sin.

> God gave them over to dishonorable passions. For their women exchanged the natural sexual relations for unnatural ones, and likewise the men also abandoned natural relations with women and were inflamed in their passions for one another. Men committed shameless acts with men and received in themselves the due penalty for their error. And just as they did not see fit to acknowledge God, God gave them over to a depraved mind, to do what should not be done. They are filled with every kind of unrighteousness, wickedness, covetousness, malice. They are rife with envy, murder, strife, deceit, hostility. They are gossips, slanderers, haters of God, insolent, arrogant, boastful, contrivers of all sorts of evil, disobedient to parents, senseless, covenant-breakers, heartless, ruthless. Although they fully know God's righteous decree that those who practice such things deserve to die, they not only do them but also approve of those who practice them (NET).

As you read those verses, did you catch the repetition of the phrase "God gave them over" (verses 26, 28; see also verse 24)? This describes how God judges people—by abandoning them to their sin, and how this sin is expressed first in sexual revolution and then in homosexual revolution. It all started in the 1960s, and since then, that is the tragic trajectory America has taken. Homosexual marriage is now the law of the land. The sexual revolution described in Romans 1:24-25 has been followed in America with shocking suddenness by the homosexual revolution described in Romans 1:26-27.

Americans have a growing sense that things are not right—that we are coming off the rails morally. In a Gallup poll, Americans were asked about their perception of moral values in the country: "How would you rate the overall state of moral values in this country—as excellent, good, only fair, or poor?"

This is how they responded:

- 45 percent said poor

- 15 percent said excellent or good

They were also asked about where they thought our moral values are headed: "Right now, do you think the state of moral values in the country as a whole is getting better or worse?"

- 76 percent said it was getting worse

- 14 percent said it was getting better

Some Americans were asked to give more details about what they perceive as moral values:

> Most commonly, respondents see a lack of respect for other people and a more general decline in moral values and standards. But the responses are quite varied. Specifically, some blame the perceived decline on poor parenting—specifically, parents not instilling proper values in their children. Some cite the poor examples of U.S. leaders in government and business who find themselves embroiled in ethical or moral scandals. And some reference larger societal factors, such as rising crime and violence, Americans turning away from God, church and religion, and the breakdown of the typical two-parent family.[5]

It is clear that America is hemorrhaging from within. Thomas Macauley, a British Parliamentarian, wrote these sobering words about the United States in 1857:

> Your Republic will be as fearfully plundered and laid waste by barbarians in the 20th century as the Roman Empire was in the 5th century, with this difference—the Huns and Vandals who ravaged the Roman Empire came from without, and your Huns and Vandals will have been engendered within your own country.[6]

It now appears that the Huns and Vandals of moral rot are upon us. When open sexual sin is condoned followed by a homosexual revolution, Romans 1 says that judgment has already begun. When people ask, "When is God going to judge America?" the answer is clear: He already is. He is judging America by abandoning her, by giving her over to her own wicked desires. How much longer until the final collapse? No one knows. But we need to be praying for our nation and doing all we can to live godly lives and promote righteousness.

Military Threat

Due to its geographic position and military might, America has enjoyed a level of peace and security most other nations envy. The United States never faced the danger of a serious attack on its own soil until December 7, 1941, and then again on September 11, 2001. Currently, the most serious external threat America faces is the nightmarish possibility of nuclear terror—a nuclear 9/11. The threat may seem far-fetched to many, but there are people who wake up every morning and think and live every day with the chief purpose of their lives being to bring havoc and ultimately nuclear devastation to America. Experts warn the threat is growing and may be more likely than not in the next decade.

Pakistan is growing more unstable all the time and has an impressive nuclear arsenal that is expected to reach 200 nukes by 2021. North Korea could weaponize its program. Iran is trying to reach the nuclear finish line and develop a deliverable nuclear weapon in spite of the nuclear deal. A nuclear device supplied by Iran could be detonated in the United States by terrorists.

While no one wants to even think about it, America would be the prime target, along with Israel, for any nuclear terrorist efforts. The horrifying threat of a nuclear 9/11 is growing. Our leaders know this and are doing all they can to stem the tide, but intelligence and military might can only do so much. It's only a matter of time until terrorists are able to get their hands on nuclear material and can detonate either a dirty bomb (which spreads harmful radiation in a city) or an actual nuclear device. Of course, either of these scenarios would cause untold loss in human life and economic catastrophe, not to mention the lingering psychological effects that may leave the nation in a state from which it will be unable to recover.

Monetary Collapse

The effects of the economic tsunami that hit the world in 2008 are still being felt. Everyone knows that the American economy is still fragile and will fail if serious changes are not implemented soon. The number of people unemployed or no longer in the work force is having a detrimental effect. Entitlement spending will doom the nation if changes are not made. It's no great surprise why America's stock is dropping. At the time of this writing,

America's national debt stands at a staggering $18.9 trillion dollars...and counting. The numbers on America's infamous debt clock near New York's Times Square have been spinning like a high-speed fan. More and more Americans are looking to the government for support. Cradle-to-grave entitlements have led to what many people dub a "nanny state." There is a popular saying that can serve as a stark reminder and warning to us: "A government big enough to give you everything you want is strong enough to take everything you have." According to the Bible, that's exactly where this all is ultimately headed under the Antichrist.

Time magazine ran an article titled "Is the Almighty Dollar Doomed?" It chronicles the growing consensus that the days of the dollar reserve system are numbered.[7]

Rich Miller and Simon Kennedy point out in their online article just how much the United States is declining on the economic front:

> "It's the passing of an era," said Robert Hormats, vice chairman of Goldman Sachs International, who helped prepare summits for presidents Gerald R. Ford, Jimmy Carter and Ronald Reagan. "The U.S. is becoming less dominant while other nations are gaining influence."[8]

According to the Office of Management and Budget, entitlement spending—Medicare, Medicaid, Social Security, and other benefit programs—now accounts for 60 percent of all spending. According to *USA Today*, "The real drivers of looming deficits are Medicare, projected to grow from $516 billion this year to $932 billion in 2018, and Social Security, forecast to grow from $581 billion this year to $966 in 2018 as Baby Boomers retire."[9]

The United States could collapse under the weight of its own excess, greed, and massive government mind-set.

Debt is not just an economic issue. It bleeds over into other key areas as well. It threatens the security (even the continued existence) of nations. For instance, the U.S. Air Force says it needs more money to maintain the U.S. dominance of the skies that it has enjoyed for decades. The American military machine is aging due to the wars in Iraq and Afghanistan, and new fighters and new technology carry a bigger and bigger price tag. If the U.S. economy hits hard enough times, money allocations will have to be prioritized, and hard decisions will have to be made. More of the limited funds going to entitlements and other government programs will mean less to defense and could leave the United States more vulnerable than ever. Past empires have fallen under the crushing weight of massive debt service and their resulting inability to fund their military. Hapsburg Spain, prerevolutionary France, the Ottoman Empire, and even the British in the buildup to World War II all went the same way.[10]

Newsweek ran a cover article on December 7, 2009, that's still compelling today. The title is "How Great Empires Fall: Steep Debt, Slow Growth and High Spending Kill Empires—and America Could Be Next." The cover had a gripping picture of the U.S. Capitol building upside down. The feature article in *Newsweek* was titled

"An Empire at Risk." Here are a few key excerpts from this insightful article by Niall Ferguson.

> We won the Cold War and weathered 9/11 but now economic weakness is endangering our global power...if the United States succumbs to a fiscal crisis, as an increasing number of economic experts fear it may, then the entire balance of global economic power could shift...If the United States doesn't come up soon with a credible plan to restore the federal budget to balance over the next 5 to 10 years, the danger is very real that a debt crisis could lead to a major weakening of American power.[11]

Ferguson notes the critical nexus between a nation's debt explosion and the inevitable weakening of its military arsenal.

> This is how empires begin to decline. It begins with a debt explosion. It ends with an inexorable reduction in the Army, Navy, and Air Force...As interest payments eat into the budget, something has to give—and that something is nearly always defense expenditure. On the Pentagon's present plan, defense spending is set to fall from above 4 percent now to 3.2 percent of GDP in 2015 and to 2.6 percent of GDP by 2028.[12]

It's known as the "arithmetic of imperial decline."[13] Without radical fiscal reform, America, unable to expend the necessary resources for its own defense, could become the next great superpower to fall irreparably on the imperial ash heap of history.

America's financial woes could also eventually lead to a much more isolationist stance. While in today's global society it's impossible not to interact economically and politically with other nations, Americans are weary of being the world's police force. With one major war just ended and another one grinding ever so slowly to a halt, and crushing debt problems, it is not difficult to envision America pulling back on the international front. If this happens, it could pave the way for the reunited Roman Empire and other nations to assume greater leadership roles, further paving the way for Antichrist's arrival.

THE RAPTURE AND THE END OF AMERICA AS WE KNOW IT

While the three scenarios we just discussed—moral meltdown, military threat, and monetary collapse— could happen alone or in a crippling combination, there's one other event that could suddenly end life in America as we know it. That event is the rapture.

When the rapture occurs, every living believer in Jesus Christ will be whisked to heaven in a moment. In the time it takes to blink your eyes, every living believer will disappear from this earth, and the bodies of God's people

who have died will be raised and rejoined with their per-
fected spirits. The rapture is vividly described in two key
New Testament passages:

> Now I say this, brethren, that flesh and blood
> cannot inherit the kingdom of God; nor does
> the perishable inherit the imperishable. Behold,
> I tell you a mystery; we will not all sleep, but
> we will all be changed, in a moment, in the
> twinkling of an eye, at the last trumpet; for
> the trumpet will sound, and the dead will be
> raised imperishable, and we will all be changed.
> For this perishable must put on the imperish-
> able, and this mortal must put on immortality
> (1 Corinthians 15:50-53).

> The Lord Himself will descend from heaven
> with a shout, with the voice of the archangel
> and with the trumpet of God, and the dead in
> Christ will rise first. Then we who are alive and
> remain will be caught up together with them in
> the clouds to meet the Lord in the air, and so we
> shall always be with the Lord. Therefore com-
> fort one another with these words (1 Thessalo-
> nians 4:16-18).

Add in the rapture to all the other surging problems,
and America will become a second-rate nation in the
twinkling of an eye. The rapture will change everything!

While every nation has believers, America has a larger percentage of believers than any other country on earth. Think about the Dow Jones the next day. The unpaid mortgages. The loss of tax revenue. The cascade of bank failures. The immediate, sudden extraction of all the salt and light from the United States may be God's final judgment on America.

The rapture will be the trigger that sets the other events of the end times in motion. After the rapture, there will be a time of further preparation as events quickly begin to line up for the commencement of the end times. Out of the chaos that ensues from the rapture, a group of ten leaders will emerge from a revived form of the Roman Empire. Eventually a strong man will emerge and begin to rise to power. The event that will catapult him to world power will be the signing of a peace agreement with Israel (more about this in the next chapter). The execution of this treaty will begin the ticking of the end-time clock as the world enters the time known as the Tribulation.

WHAT CAN WE DO?

No one on earth knows when the rapture will occur and America will fall. In the meantime, we must never forget to follow God's domestic policy for our nation by praying earnestly for our nation and leaders (1 Timothy 2:1-2) and living righteous lives (Proverbs 14:34), and to fulfill God's foreign policy by sharing the good news with the nations (Romans 10:15) and blessing the Jewish people (Genesis 12:1-3). We must remember that ultimately, the fate of a nation is not dependent upon politics, military might, or economics, but on righteousness, goodness, and mercy.

In recent years, America has placed itself on slippery ground by undermining its support for Israel. While America is not obligated to agree with every policy decision Israel makes, the Scripture is clear that nations are cursed or blessed by God based on their treatment of the Jewish people. History has borne this out. I like to say that every time someone has tried to wipe out the Jewish people, the Jews end up with a holiday. With Pharaoh they got Passover, with Haman in the book of Esther they got Purim, with Antiochus Epiphanes they got Hanukkah, and with Hitler they got May 14, 1948, the rebirth of the modern nation of Israel. Long ago, God promised that those who bless Abraham and his descendants will be blessed, and that those who curse them will be cursed (Genesis 12:3). God has never abrogated this promise. Much of America's blessing as a nation can be traced to its benevolent treatment of the Jews and Israel, which has waned dramatically under President Obama. In 2009, he publicly demanded that Israel halt all settlement activity as a condition for further talks with the Palestinians, a demand that the Palestinian negotiator Mahmoud Abbas had not even made. Obama also announced demands on Israel at the United Nations, contributing to "the atmosphere of menace toward Israel" at the Israel-despising body.[14]

In May 2011, in his most egregious betrayal of Israel, President Obama called on the Jewish nation to return to the 1967 borders as the basis for the creation of a neighboring Palestinian State. This statement put the United States squarely at odds with Israel. Israeli Prime Minister Netanyahu responded quickly and forthrightly:

> While Israel is prepared to make generous compromises for peace, it cannot go back to the 1967 lines. These lines are indefensible. Remember that, before 1967, Israel was all of nine miles wide...It was half the width of the Washington Beltway. And these were not the boundaries of peace; they were the boundaries of repeated wars, because the attack on Israel was so attractive.[15]

I heard one Israeli official refer to the 1967 borders as "Auschwitz borders."

One of the surest ways for America to seal its doom is to turn its back on Israel and force that nation into a no-win situation. Again, while support of Israel doesn't mean a rubber stamp for every policy decision they make, stating that they must return to the 1967 borders as a condition for peace is a nonstarter. As Mona Charen said about President Obama's posture toward Israel, "A false friend can do more damage than an open enemy."[16] America must remain a staunch supporter and faithful ally to Israel. One of the secrets to the nation's greatness in spite of all its other failures has been its longtime support of

Israel, and God has sent blessing upon this country as He promised He would to anyone who supported Israel. If America continues on its current path and fails to bless the Jewish people, the final vestige of God's blessing could be withdrawn, and the end could come like a flood.

Pray for our nation!

Pray for our leaders!

CHAPTER 8

The Coming Middle East Peace

"If an expert says it can't be done, get another expert."[1]

David Ben-Gurion

What is the one issue in our world today that often overshadows all others? What is the one problem that has festered in the world's side for decades? What is the one issue that finds its way into the world's newspapers and television news reports constantly? The ongoing hostilities in the Middle East. The Mideast peace process. The "road map to peace." This one continuing crisis monopolizes world attention.

Peace has always been a scarce commodity in the Middle East. Have you ever wondered why? Certainly there are political and humanitarian reasons for the world's interest in this ongoing struggle. But I believe there's more to it than that. The fact peace has been so elusive in the Middle East is a key sign of the times. The

Bible says that the event that signals the beginning of the seven-year Tribulation is the signing of a peace treaty or covenant between the leader of the end-time Western Confederacy, the Antichrist, and the nation of Israel (Daniel 9:27). The current turmoil and yearning for peace in the Middle East is setting the stage for this covenant of peace between Antichrist and Israel.

ISIS continues to wreak havoc, further heightening the cry for peace. Israel could feel compelled at some point to attack Iran if it violates the nuclear deal. A regional war could erupt, serving as the final catalyst for this comprehensive peace agreement predicted in Scripture. Syria is embroiled in a bloodbath. Egypt is unsettled. The Palestinians and Hezbollah are a constant threat to Israel. They will be hammered if they retaliate against Israel for striking Iran. Whatever unfolds in the days ahead, Israel will certainly be ready for a respite. Israel's neighbors may want a reset. Iran might even be willing to sign on to some peace agreement to give it time to rearm if Israel were to damage its nuclear facilities. The hoofbeats of war we hear today could be the precursor to peace in the future—a peace that's been many years in the making.

THE PHANTOM OF PEACE

The genesis of the modern peace process in the Middle East began about ninety years ago. The two main parties in this effort were Emir Faisal, the son of the sherif of

Mecca and Medina, and Chaim Weizmann, the leader of world Zionism, who later became the first president of Israel. These men forged an agreement in 1918, but it never really got off the ground because of a lack of French and British support.

The peace process has been swimming upstream now for more than 60 years. Since the official foundation of Israel as a nation on May 14, 1948, there has been one long war sprinkled with a perpetual peace process between Israel and her Arab neighbors. There has been no real or lasting peace—only brief periods of no war.

The Arab nations surrounding Israel have been in a declared state of war with the Jewish nation since May 14, 1948. Only Egypt and Jordan currently have peace with Israel. Here is a brief sketch of the ongoing hostilities between Israel and her neighbors.

1948-49	When Israel officially became an independent state on May 14, 1948, she was immediately attacked from all sides by Egypt, Jordan, Iraq, Syria, Lebanon, and Saudi Arabia. When the truce was implemented on January 7, 1949, Israel had expanded her territory from 5000 square miles to 8000, including much of the Negev, the huge desert to the south between Israel and Egypt.
1956	The Suez War between Egypt and Israel. Egyptian leader Gamal Abdel Nasser nationalized the Suez Canal. On October 29, 1956, Israel invaded the Sinai Peninsula and took control. Later, Israel returned the Sinai to Egypt.

1964	The Palestinian Liberation Organization (PLO) was formed with the dual purpose of creating a Palestinian State and destroying Israel.
1967	The famous "Six-Day War" (June 5–10). Israel captured the Sinai Peninsula from Egypt, the West Bank from Jordan, the Golan Heights from Syria, and seized control of Jerusalem.
1973	The Yom Kippur War. At 2:00 p.m., on October 6, 1973, on Israel's most holy day, the Day of Atonement (Yom Kippur), Israel was attacked by Egypt and Syria. After heavy fighting, Israel repelled the invaders.
1982–85	The war with Lebanon.
1987–93	The First Palestinian Intifada (uprising) in Gaza. This uprising ended in 1993 with the signing of the Oslo Accords, signed by the prime minister of Israel, Yitzhak Rabin, and the PLO leader, Yasser Arafat.
2000	The Second Palestinian Intifada began in September 2000 when Ariel Sharon visited the Temple Mount. In this uprising, the Palestinians employed suicide (homicide) bombers.
2003	The U.S. presented the "road map" for peace in the Middle East.
2005	Israel withdraws from all 21 settlements in the Gaza Strip.
2006	Israel wages a bloody 34-day War with Hezbollah.
1979–2016	The shadow war between Israel and Iran.

As you can see, the brief history of modern Israel is a history of war, and repeated, futile attempts to achieve peace. Will a war with Iran be next?

NICE TRY

The United States, the Soviet Union, the United Nations, and various European nations have all given the Middle East peace process their best shot—over and over again. And for the most part, they have failed. In the United States, virtually every president and secretary of state since 1948 has worked at peace, only to come up short again and again. Despite great, well-meaning effort, the world has failed to make any real, lasting headway in the ongoing hostilities between Israel and her neighbors.

The United States was able to broker peace treaties between Israel and her two neighbors, Egypt and Jordan. Nevertheless, both of these nations continue to harbor deep animosity toward Israel, and they often side with other Arab nations in issues involving conflict with Israel. The Oslo Accords, signed on September 13, 1993, on the White House lawn by Yitzhak Rabin and Yasser Arafat, brought great hope. But the second intifada (uprising) that began on September 26, 2000, between Israel and the Palestinians and the 2006 war with Hezbollah in Lebanon and Hamas in Gaza dashed all the hopes raised by the Oslo Accords.

The Arab Spring has also left lingering questions
about the future between Israel and Egypt. Most Egyptians today want to see the 1979 peace treaty with Israel
scrapped.[2] The southern flank of Israel could be reopened
as a war zone at some point. The showdown with Iran is
at its worst. ISIS has unleashed its horror. We often wonder if peace will ever come to the Middle East, and how it
could possibly be brought about.

Peace Is Coming

The Bible speaks of a future peace treaty for Israel that
will be brokered by the coming Antichrist—this is one of
the most important events of the end times. According
to Scripture, the Antichrist will rise up from a reunited,
revived Roman Empire that will probably be centered in
Europe. The European Union could be the embryonic
stages of this power bloc.

The peace treaty the Antichrist forges will bring a false,
counterfeit, temporary peace. It won't last, but for a while
it will look like the world's dream for peace in the Middle
East will finally have been realized.

I believe this treaty will come about after the rapture,
when all believers in Jesus Christ are already to heaven.
This chart helps put the events of the end times in order.

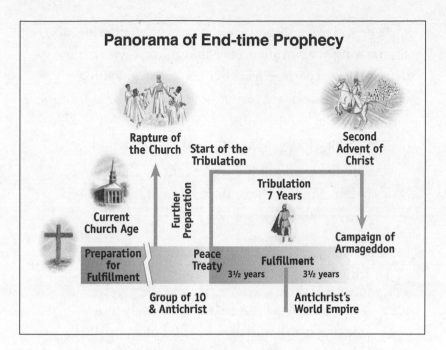

Panorama of End-time Prophecy

Rapture of
the Church   Start of the
              Tribulation

Second
Advent of
Christ

Current
Church Age

Further
Preparation

Tribulation
7 Years

Campaign of
Armageddon

Preparation
for
Fulfillment

Peace
Treaty

Fulfillment
3½ years

Fulfillment
3½ years

Group of 10
& Antichrist

Antichrist's
World Empire

*Here is a visual time line that depicts the sequence of events
before and during the Tribulation.*[3]

Adapted and used with permission of Tim LaHaye and Thomas Ice, *Charting the End Times* (Eugene, OR: Harvest House, 2001). The chart above is based on charts that appear in LaHaye and Ice's book, with one adaptation. The placement of the Group of 10 and Antichrist before the signing of the peace treaty rather than after.

There are two main Old Testament passages that indicate that there will be some kind of peace settlement for Israel at the beginning of the coming seven-year Tribulation. I believe that both of these passages refer to the same peace treaty that will be signed at the very beginning of the Tribulation. The first is Daniel 9:27, which says, "And he [Antichrist] will make a firm covenant with the many for one week [7 years], but in the middle of the week he will put a stop to sacrifice and grain offering; and on the wing of abominations will come one who makes desolate." This passage teaches us at least 5 key things about this future peace treaty:

- It will be between Israel and the Antichrist, but will almost certainly involve others. This seems to indicate that the reunited Roman Empire will be a key player.

- It will begin the final 7-year time of the Tribulation.

- It will be a "firm" covenant, which may indicate that it will initially be forced or compelled. It may be a "take it or leave it" deal for Israel and its neighbors.

- It will eventually give Jews the right to offer sacrifices in a rebuilt temple, which means a Jewish temple must be rebuilt.

- It will be temporary and short-lived. The agreement will be broken by the Antichrist himself at the midpoint in one of the great double-crosses of all time.

Charles Dyer, a respected prophecy teacher and author, summarizes the nature of the Daniel 9:27 covenant:

What is this "covenant" that the Antichrist will make with Israel? Daniel does not specify its content, but he does indicate that it will extend for seven years. During the first half of this time Israel feels at peace and secure, so the covenant must provide some guarantee for Israel's national security. Very likely the covenant will allow Israel to be at peace with her Arab neighbors. One result of the covenant is that Israel will be allowed to rebuild her temple in Jerusalem. This world ruler will succeed where Kissinger, Carter, Reagan, Bush, and other world leaders have failed. He will be known as the man of peace![4]

The second Old Testament text that speaks of Israel's end-time peace agreement is Ezekiel 38:8, which says that "in the latter years" Israel will be "living securely, all of them." Then verse 11 says that Israel will be "at rest" and will "live securely." According to Ezekiel, there will be a time in the latter years when the regathered people of Israel will be living in a time of great peace and prosperity. During this time, when Israel has let down her guard, a coalition of nations led by Russia and Iran will invade the land and be wiped out by God. We will look at that in more detail in the next chapter. But it's safe to say that what we see today, and have witnessed over the last few decades of the Middle East peace process, points toward this key end-time event that will kick-start the final seven years of this age.

How Much Longer?

What form will the coming peace settlement take? In view of the many surprises, twists, and turns that have taken place in the Middle East, it is hazardous to guess the precise form of such a peace settlement. It is also difficult to predict what catastrophic events will make this forced peace necessary. Certainly the rise of ISIS has made peace in the Middle East more attractive to all parties. But the outbreak of war as a result of an Israeli pre-emptive strike against Iran could be the event that drives the parties to the peace table. It could even be an all-out Middle East war involving the use of tactical nuclear weapons. An Israeli attack against Iran and the Iranian counterstrike through its proxies in Gaza and Lebanon could form part of the backdrop.

Perhaps conditions in the Middle East will deteriorate so rapidly under ISIS that a strong military presence will be necessary to restore order. Or perhaps a peace settlement would be accepted by Israel's enemies for a temporary position of advantage in preparation for a possible later war with Israel, as we see in Ezekiel 38–39.

Whatever the reason, the world must be in danger of self-destruction. Otherwise, Israel and the nations of the world would not surrender power to the new leaders of the revived Roman Empire.

Whatever the precipitating events, ultimately the peace agreement must give Israel security from attack and freedom from having to be in a constant state of military alert to defend and protect itself. It is very possible that

an international peacekeeping force and secure boundaries may be guaranteed by the new and powerful leader
who signs the agreement. A general disarmament in the
area may also be part of the treaty. In the aftermath of
Israel's indecisive war with Hezbollah in the summer of
2006, Israel was willing to allow a peacekeeping force, led
by European Union forces, to guarantee the security of its
northern border. Israel's agreement to have a U.N. peacekeeping force control southern Lebanon could be a prelude to its willingness to give over more and more of its
security to the West.

THE TREATY AND THE TEMPLE

The key issue in Middle East peace negotiations will
be the city of Jerusalem itself, which Israel prizes more
than any other possession. Undoubtedly there will be a
strong attempt to maintain Jerusalem as an international
city, with free access not only for Jews but for Christians and Muslims as well. The temple area may end up
becoming internationalized, and Israel's territorial conquests will be greatly reduced.

With the rise of radical Islamic terrorism and the
changing role of the United States as the sole supporting
force behind Israel's continuity as a nation, it seems that
any settlement that does not deal with Jerusalem will not
satisfy the Arab world.

How soon will such a peace settlement come? No one
can predict. But come it must—here the Scriptures are

emphatic. There will be a treaty between the new world leader and Israel (Daniel 9:27) that will permit Israel to continue and to renew her religious ceremonies, including the building of a Jewish temple and the reactivation of Jewish sacrifices. All of this was anticipated in the prophecies of Daniel 9:27 and 12:11 and was implied in Christ's own prophecy relating to the stopping of the sacrifices when the treaty is broken (Matthew 24:15).

How it could ever become possible for this temple to be rebuilt is one of the thorniest problems in all of Bible prophecy. How can the Jews rebuild their temple with the Dome of the Rock and the Al-Aqsa mosque sitting on the Temple Mount? Many solutions to this problem have been proposed. But never forget that before 1948, people thought it was impossible for the Jewish people to ever be restored to their ancient homeland. Yet today almost 40 percent of the Jews in the world now live in Israel, and incredibly, almost two-thirds of them now want to see the temple rebuilt.

Ynetnews reported the startling findings of a new poll about the temple on July 30, 2009. The poll asked respondents whether they wanted to see the temple rebuilt:

> Sixty-four percent responded favorably, while 36% said no. An analysis of the answers showed that not only the ultra-Orthodox and the religious look forward to the rebuilding of the Temple (100% and 97% respectively), but also

the traditional public (91%) and many seculars—47%...The Temple was destroyed 1,942
years ago, and almost two-thirds of the population want to see it rebuilt, including 47% of
seculars.[5]

This groundswell of support for a third Jewish temple
is another key sign of the times. For years, groups like the
Temple Mount Faithful and others have championed and
even made preparations for the rebuilding of the temple,
but broad public support seemed woefully lacking. That
appears to have changed—drastically. The temple must
be in place during the Tribulation period for the Antichrist to take his seat in it and defile it (as predicted in
2 Thessalonians 2:4), and for sacrifices to be reinstituted.

While no one knows when the temple will be rebuilt
or how it will be accomplished, the stage setting for its
appearance and the coming treaty of peace continues.
The emergence of ISIS and the Israel-Iran showdown may
be critical elements that lead to bringing the nations to
the bargaining table for a comprehensive Middle East
peace.

CHAPTER 9

The Times of the Signs

"The study of history and prophecy as it relates to the nations is especially appropriate at this point in the twentieth century when history seems to be moving rapidly toward its destiny. Only the divine interpretation of history and the divine revelation of the prophetic future of nations can give us a sure light in these troubled times." [1]

John F. Walvoord, *The Nations in Prophecy* (1967)

Some signs are easier to read than others. This is especially true when traveling to a foreign country. Meaning often gets "lost in translation." Here are a few signs in other countries translated into English:

In a Paris elevator: "Please leave your values at the front desk."

In a hotel in Athens: "Visitors are expected to complain at the office between the hours of 9 and 11 a.m. daily."

In an Austrian hotel catering to skiers: "Not to perambulate the corridors during the hours of repose in the boots of ascension."

In a Rhodes tailor shop: "Order your summers suit. Because is a big rush we will execute customers in strict rotation."

In an advertisement by a Hong Kong dentist: "Teeth extracted by the latest Methodists."

In a Copenhagen airline ticket office: "We take your bags and send them in all directions." [Yes, they do!]

In an Acapulco hotel: "The manager has personally passed all the water served here."

In a Tokyo shop: "Our nylons cost more than common, but you'll find they are best in the long run."[2]

It's true. Some signs are clearer than others. Some are straightforward and easy to read, while others are more difficult to decipher. Jesus chided the people in His day for failing to discern the signs of the times of His first advent (Matthew 16:1-3). He told us that clear signs will portend His second advent (Matthew 24:4-31; Luke 21:25).

Make no mistake. The prophecies of the Bible will be fulfilled. Just as hundreds of past prophecies have been fulfilled literally just as the Bible predicted, we know that the unfulfilled prophecies will also come to pass literally. The Bible has a proven track record. The only question is, *When* will God bring them to pass? We can watch today as the various players assume their roles and the necessary scenes move into place on the set. We can watch the buildup as it happens.

WHAT TO WATCH FOR

In the pages of Scripture, God has given us some "signs of the times" that are clear if we will look for them. What are some of the signs we should be looking for? Which events on the horizon today point toward what lies ahead? Let me mention five specific signposts on the road to the Battle of Gog and Magog and beyond.

The Regathering of Israel

One unmistakable sign is the rebirth of the modern state of Israel and the regathering of the Jewish people to their ancient homeland. Since 1948, this signpost has been in place. This is often referred to as the super sign of the end times, since so many other end-time prophecies hinge on the presence of the Jewish people in their land. Israel is at the center of God's end-time agenda. Almost 40 percent of the Jews in the world now live in Israel. The hundreds of ancient prophecies about the end-time

restoration of the Jewish people to their land are coming
to fruition before our eyes. This piece of the prophetic
puzzle must be in place for the end times to commence,
and it has been in place for almost 70 years.

The Reuniting of the Roman Empire

The Scriptures predict in Daniel 2 and 7 and Revelation 13 and 17 that the Roman Empire will be revived
or reunited in the end times. It will begin as a confederation of nations ruled over by ten kings or leaders, like
a ruling committee or oligarchy (Daniel 7:7,24). These
ten leaders are pictured as ten toes on the image in Daniel 2 and ten horns on a beast in Daniel 7. I like to call
this the Group of Ten, or G-10. Later this group will give
its authority to one man, the little horn in Daniel 7:8. He
will consolidate power in the area of the historical Roman
Empire, probably including North Africa and Western
Asia as well as the core of his empire in Europe. In the
final phase of this end-time Roman Empire, this Western leader, known in the New Testament as the Antichrist
or Beast, will extend his rule to the entire world. His
global kingdom will last for the final half (three-and-a-
half years) of what the Bible calls the Tribulation. He and
his kingdom will be suddenly and completely destroyed
when the Lord Jesus Christ returns to earth.

This second signpost is not fully in place yet because
the reunited Roman Empire is not ruled over by ten leaders. Yet we can watch current developments in Europe

with great interest. The Bible predicts that when these ten leaders and the nations they represent come together, it won't be easy. It will be like trying to mix iron and clay (Daniel 2:42-43). This mention of iron and clay, or inherent strength and weakness at the same time, is reflected in the European Union today. The European Union has great economic and political clout, but its diversity in culture, language, and politics is also ever-present. It represents the joining of strong nations with weak ones, just as Daniel predicted. This corresponds to what we see developing today. One can easily see how the European Union could develop into the feet and toes of iron and clay.

The Road to Peace

The third signpost, as we discussed in chapter 8, is the worldwide cry for peace. As everyone knows, the world today is in the throes of struggle and conflict, primarily centered in the Middle East, with Israel at the vortex. The Bible predicts that a time of peace is coming for Israel and even briefly for the entire world (1 Thessalonians 5:1-3).

The Rise of Globalism

The fourth significant signpost is the dramatic move toward globalization. The end-time prophecy of a one-world government and economy, prophesied in Revelation 13 and 17, looks more and more like a mirror of our modern society. Our world is shrinking fast. Exponential technological advances have torn down walls between governments and economies and have exposed everyone to immediate access to information.

Scripture foresaw this exact scenario in Revelation 13, where one man will eventually seize world power, establishing a worldwide kingdom for the first time since the days just after the flood under Nimrod (Genesis 10–11). The sudden, stunning rise of globalism is a sure sign of the times.

The Reduction of America

The United States is strangely absent from the prophetic Scriptures. As we noted in chapter 7, this silence is significant. In the end times, world power will be concentrated in a Western confederacy headed by the Antichrist. This alliance will eventually dominate the world landscape (Revelation 13:4). This being the case, America will not be the world leader during the end times. What will happen to America is not known with certainty, but the current slide of American power and influence is paving the way for greater globalism and the rise of other international alliances to power, just as Scripture predicts.

The Relentless War in the Middle East

The sixth significant sign of the end times is the seemingly endless Middle East crisis. Everyone knows that pressure is building in the Middle East. The lid could blow off at any time. How much longer can the tensions be held in check? Anyone who follows the news, even casually, knows that the Middle East is engulfed in the fires of mayhem and even genocide. Egypt is weak and unstable. Syria has descended into complete chaos. Iran threatens to wipe Israel off the map and continues to test ballistic missiles that can carry a nuclear payload. ISIS is a Middle East and global menace. The Middle East is ready to go off, and the only answer is a comprehensive peace treaty like the one predicted in Scripture.

PUTTING THE PIECES TOGETHER

Never before in human history has there been such a convergence of trends and developments that are part of the matrix of end-time events predicted in Scripture. The major actors are already in the wings waiting for their moment on center stage. The necessary props are moving into place. The prophetic play could begin any moment. The Middle East dominates the attention of the world. Dominoes are falling and the landscape of the Middle East continues to morph before our eyes. The Jewish people are regathering and surviving. The Russian bear has emerged from its brief hibernation and is flexing its muscles all over the Middle East. Iran is rising and has not abandoned its nuclear goal. Europe, although currently struggling, is uniting. The United States is declining economically and politically, paving the way for the rise of greater globalism. The world is clamoring for peace. And world events have never before had such an immediate, instantaneous impact. Decades ago, some events would have taken months or even years to bring about change. But now, these same kinds of events take minutes. The stunning pace of change and the incredible acceleration of impact and effect create a sense in all of us that we are moving toward a great crisis. Events are happening so quickly that it's difficult to keep up.

So far in this book, we have considered a few of the events the Bible predicts for the future of the Middle East and the world, and we have attempted to relate current events to what the Scriptures prophesy. At this point, I want to try to bring it all together—to bring these events into tight focus.

From my study of Bible prophecy, here's my best effort at this time to put the pieces together. Here's a sequence of ten key events that I see looming on the horizon.

1. World tensions will continue to build. The world will continue to turn against Israel as she struggles for survival in a sea of enemies. Israel, Islam, terror, the threat of nuclear jihad, rolling Middle East revolutions, and oil will dominate world news, riveting world focus on the Middle East. The Israel-Iran crisis will eventually erupt into war, possibly escalating into a regional war. Worldwide recession may ensue. The global cry for peace, security, and stability will reach a deafening crescendo.

2. Someday, without any warning, Jesus will come to take His bride to heaven. All believers in Christ will be whisked away to the Father's house in heaven. All unbelievers will be left behind. This event, known as the rapture, will come without any warning. Other events *may* precede it, but no events *must* precede it. It can happen at any moment. It's not necessarily immediate—happening in the next moment—but it is imminent. It could happen at any moment. The rapture will serve as the prophetic trigger that will unleash a series of events predicted in Scripture for the end times.

3. The United States will be greatly affected by the rapture, losing millions of its citizens. In the wake of the rapture and its devastating results on the U.S. economy, world power will shift dramatically away from the United States to Europe and Asia.

4. Out of the chaos and confusion created by the rapture, the Antichrist will rise from a reunited form of the Roman Empire led by an oligarchy or ruling committee consisting of ten leaders. This revived or reunited Roman Empire will probably be some future form of what today is called the European Union. And the ultimate leader of this empire will make a seven-year peace treaty with Israel, ushering in a brief

season of worldwide peace (Ezekiel 38:8,11; Daniel 9:27; 1 Thessalonians 5:1-3; Revelation 6:1-2). The world will enter into a kind of new *Pax Romana* (Roman Peace).

5. In brokering the Middle East peace deal, the Antichrist will temporarily end the threat of terror and instability and guarantee the uninterrupted flow of oil to the West. He will be hailed as a great peacemaker. At last, it will appear that the world has what it has long waited for—peace and prosperity.

6. This global utopia won't last long. Sometime during the first half of the Tribulation, the coalition of nations in Ezekiel 38 will stage a surprise attack on Israel when she has let down her guard. Russia's expanding power, influence, and alliances in the Middle East will be the hooks in the jaws that will drag her reluctantly into this course of action. The attack will be against both Israel and the West, since Israel will be joined to the Antichrist by her treaty. By this invasion of Israel, Russia, Iran, Turkey, Libya, Sudan, the nations of Central Asia, Egypt, and possibly other nations will hope to draw the West into open confrontation—or a final great clash of civilizations.

7. God will supernaturally intervene, just like in Old Testament times, to miraculously rescue Israel from total annihilation and destroy the invaders.

8. The power vacuum created by the destruction of the armies of Russia, Iran, and most of the other Islamic nations will be quickly filled by the Antichrist. He will seize this opportunity to invade Israel, breaking his covenant. Then he will move against the helpless nations of Egypt, Libya, and Sudan as he launches his world empire at the midpoint of the seven-year Tribulation. He will establish a headquarters in Babylon (modern Iraq) and seize control of the great oil supply in the Persian Gulf.

9. The Great Tribulation Jesus spoke of in Matthew 24:21 will break out, plunging the world into its final days of darkness and dismay.

10. The world will be saved from the brink of destruction by the second coming of Jesus Christ. Jesus will then establish His 1000-year kingdom of peace and righteousness on the earth.

In a book I helped update, titled *Armageddon, Oil, and Terror*, John Walvoord and I included this "Prophetic

Checklist for the Nations." I thought it might be helpful to include it here.

A Prophetic Checklist for the Nations

The prophetic events related to the nations can be compiled chronologically. Consider how the following list of significant world events—past, present, and future—shows that the world is being dramatically prepared for end-time events.

1. The establishment of the United Nations began a serious first step toward world government.

2. The rebuilding of Europe after World War II made a revival of the Roman Empire possible.

3. Israel was reestablished as a nation.

4. Russia rose to world power and became the ally of the Islamic world.

5. The Common Market and World Bank showed the need for some international regulation of the world economy.

6. China rose to world power and developed the capacity to field a massive army.

7. The Middle East became the most significant trouble spot in the world.

8. The oil blackmail awakened the world to the new concentration of wealth and power in the Middle East.

9. The Iron Curtain fell, removing the final barrier to the revival of the Roman Empire.

10. The world clamors for peace because of the continued disruption caused by the high price of oil, terrorist incidents, and the confused military situation in the Middle East.

11. Ten leaders (the "Group of Ten") will emerge from a European and Mediterranean Coalition—beginnings of the last stage of the prophetic fourth-world empire.

12. In a dramatic power play, a new Mediterranean leader will uproot three leaders of the coalition and take control of the powerful ten-leader group.

13. The new Mediterranean leader will negotiate a "final" peace settlement in the Middle East (broken three-and-a-half years later).

14. Russia and her Islamic allies will attempt an invasion of Israel but will be miraculously destroyed.

15. The Mediterranean leader will proclaim himself

world dictator, break his peace settlement with Israel, and declare himself to be God.

16. The new world dictator will desecrate the temple in Jerusalem.

17. The terrible judgments of the great Tribulation will be poured out on the nations of the world.

18. Worldwide rebellion will threaten the world dictator's rule as armies from all over the globe converge on the Middle East for World War III.

19. Christ will return to earth with His armies from heaven.

20. The armies of the world will unite to resist Christ's coming and will be destroyed in the Battle of Armageddon.

21. Christ will establish His millennial reign on earth, ending the times of the Gentiles.[3]

You have to admit—that's quite a forecast. The earth appears to be on the verge of entering into its most dangerous and difficult days. We all need to be praying regularly for Israel and the people of the Middle East. The people there are in the grip of false religion and brutal dictators who oppress and take advantage of them. This is all the more reason the church must seek to reach all of the Middle East and North Africa with the gospel of

Jesus Christ before it is too late. Please be praying faithfully for the dear people in these nations at this critical hour.

Another critical thing that each of us needs to do is pause and consider where we stand personally with the Lord. Nothing we can do is more important. The Middle East faces a crisis that could easily erupt into a regional war or something even worse. Certainly the already-wobbly world economy will take a major hit. People everywhere will be affected.

We live in uncertain times, and the prophetic signposts seem to be aligning, just as the Bible predicted. Where will you go when the rapture occurs? Will you be taken or left behind? Or what will happen to you if you die first? This is the question of utmost importance for every person.

CHAPTER 10

Do Not Let Your Heart Be Troubled

"Do not let your heart be troubled; believe in God,
believe also in Me. In My Father's house are many
dwelling places; if it were not so, I would have told you;
for I go to prepare a place for you. If I go and prepare
a place for you, I will come again and receive you to
Myself, that where I am, there you may be also."

Jesus Christ (John 14:1-3)

Years ago, the noted English agnostic Thomas Huxley was in Dublin, Ireland, for some speaking engagements. On one occasion, he left his hotel in a hurry to catch a train, taking one of the city's famous horse-drawn taxis. Huxley thought that the doorman at the hotel had told the driver where he was going, so he simply settled back in the cab and told the man at the reins to drive fast. The driver set off at a furious pace. In a few minutes,

Huxley realized that the cab was headed away from the station. "Do you know where you're going?" he shouted to the driver. "No, your honor," the driver answered, "but I'm driving fast."

This story sums up the spirit of our own tumultuous, troubled times. There is furious motion, great speed, yet few seem to know where they are or where they're headed. For our modern world, life is like Franklin Delano Roosevelt described it in his first inaugural address: "We don't know where we are going but we are on our way."[1] That's an apt picture of what is happening today.

But as we've seen, we can know where we're going. We don't know everything that's coming, but we can see that the specific signposts that point to the end times are lining up. The stage is being set for the opening act of the most astonishing drama of history. As we watch the Middle East simmer, boil, and explode, it appears that the curtain could go up at any time and the drama could begin.

What should our response be to all of this? Should we fold in fear? Or wither in worry?

It's critical for us to remember that God did not give us Bible prophecy to *scare* us but to *prepare* us. He didn't give it to us to make us *anxious*, but to make us *aware*. So, how should we prepare for what's coming? How should you respond? Your response depends on where you stand with the Lord.

What Prophecy Means to the Unbeliever

A Scottish surgeon named Sir James Simpson was one of Queen Victoria's trusted royal physicians. The Scottish people loved Dr. Simpson deeply—so much so that when this godly man died, 80,000 Scots honored him by watching his funeral procession make its way through Edinburgh.

In 1847, Dr. Simpson made an important discovery. While conducting experiments with chloroform, he realized that this organic compound would make it possible for doctors to perform operations without causing pain to their patients. This was a very significant development toward modernizing medicine.

Later in his life, Simpson was giving a lecture at the University of Edinburgh. A student in the audience asked him what he considered his most important accomplishment. The students thought he would probably point to the research that led him to realize chloroform could have value in the medical realm. To the surprise of the students, Dr. Simpson replied, "My most valuable discovery was when I discovered myself a sinner and that Jesus Christ was my Savior."[2] Not long afterward, when the surgeon was dying in extreme pain, he commented, "When I think, it is of the words 'Jesus only,' and really, that is all that is needed, is it not?"

Have you made life's greatest discovery? Have you come to realize that you are a sinner and that Jesus Christ is your Savior? Have you found that "Jesus only" is all that you need for salvation from your sins? If not, why not trust Him now?

No person knows how much time he has left on this earth, either personally or prophetically. Personally, all of us are painfully aware of our mortality. We have no guarantee we will see tomorrow. Prophetically, Christ could come at any moment to take His bride, the church, to heaven, and all unbelievers will be left behind to endure the horrors of the Tribulation period.

With this in mind, the most important question you could answer in all of life is whether or not you have a personal relationship with Jesus Christ as Savior. That's because the way you answer will determine where you spend all of eternity.

The message of salvation through Jesus Christ contains both bad news and good news. The bad news is that the Bible declares that all people, including you and me, are sinful and therefore separated from the Holy God of the universe (Isaiah 59:2; Romans 3:23). God is holy and cannot just overlook sin. A just payment for the debt must be made. But we are spiritually bankrupt, and we have no resources within ourselves to pay the huge debt we owe.

The good news (or the gospel) is that Jesus Christ has come and satisfied our sin debt. He bore our judgment and paid the price for our sins. He died on the cross for our sins and was raised to life on the third day to prove conclusively that the work of salvation had been fully accomplished. Colossians 2:14 says that He "canceled out the certificate of debt consisting of decrees against us, which was hostile to us; and He has taken it out of the way, having nailed it to the cross." First Peter 3:18 says, "Christ also died for sins once for all, the just for the unjust, so that He might bring us to God."

The salvation that Christ accomplished for us is available to all through faith in Jesus Christ. Salvation from sin is a free gift that God offers to sinful people who deserve judgment. Won't you receive the gift today? Place your faith and trust in Christ and in Him alone for your eternal salvation. The Bible makes it crystal clear:

- "Believe in the Lord Jesus, and you will be saved" (Acts 16:31).

- "As many as received Him, to them He gave the right to become children of God, even to those who believe in His name" (John 1:12).

Now that you know the truth of the rapture and that those who fail to trust Christ will be left behind to endure the terrible horrors of the Tribulation, won't you respond to the invitation before it is too late?

Accept Christ personally by calling upon Him to save you from your sins. You can do it right now, right where you are. Make sure you're ready when Jesus comes!

What Prophecy Means to the Believer

God spent a great deal of time and ink telling us what to expect in the future. One out of every thirteen verses in the New Testament relates to the coming of Christ. Our Lord's coming is mentioned more than 300 times in the 260 chapters of the New Testament. So, clearly, it's important. But while it's key that we hold this truth, it's equally important that this truth hold us. That it makes a practical difference in how we live each day. That it motivates us to live godly lives in the present.

Every key New Testament prophetic passage contains practical application closely associated with it. Prophecy was not given just to stir our imagination or capture our attention. Prophecy is intended by God to change our attitudes and actions so that we are more in line with His Word and His character.

Prophecy expert Charles Dyer emphasizes this purpose of Bible prophecy:

> God gave prophecy to change our hearts, not to fill our heads with knowledge. God never predicted future events just to satisfy our curiosity about the future. Every time God announces events that are future, He includes with His predictions practical applications to life. God's pronouncements about the future carry with them specific advice for the "here and now."[3]

According to the Bible, there are many life-changing effects or influences that understanding the future is to have on our hearts. Here are five key ones for us to apply:

We Have Hope and Peace in Troubled Times

I had the privilege of attending the Fiesta Bowl with my family in January 2012 to watch our alma mater, the Oklahoma State University Cowboys, play the Stanford Cardinal. Oklahoma State fell down early 14-0 but came roaring back. The game was exciting and nerve-racking. Stanford missed a late chip shot field goal to seal the victory, and the game went into overtime. Stanford got the ball first and missed another field goal. With the ball on the one-yard line, Oklahoma State kicked a field goal, pulling out the victory in stunning fashion.

When we got back to our room later that night, my sons and I turned on the television, and the channel was replaying the game we had just finished watching a few hours earlier. We sat down to watch it, and I have to say that I was much more relaxed when I was viewing the rerun. Even when OSU fell behind on numerous occasions, I was totally relaxed. No sweat. Why? I already knew the outcome. I knew that we had won. None of the setbacks, turnovers, or missed opportunities during the rebroadcast caused me the least bit of anxiety. I knew how the game would end. I even went to bed before the rerun was over.

There's something about knowing the outcome in advance that brings us peace and rest. The same should be true of our lives now. While we don't know every detail of what's ahead, we do know who wins. The final score is already in the Book. Knowing what's ahead gives us hope, comfort, and confidence in a troubled, uncertain world.

People everywhere are drowning in discouragement and uncertainty. Many feel as if they've lost control of their destiny. They seem more downcast, discouraged, and even more depressed than ever before. News on every front is troubling: Political impotence and irresponsibility exist in our government, economic fear and uncertainty continues, and wars and rumors of wars are spreading all over the world. Added to these problems are the personal trials and difficulties we all face. Trouble is the common denominator of all mankind. Yet, even in a world where the Niagara of bad news never seems to end, we have hope. We know how the story ends. God has given us glimpses of the future to reassure us that He is in total control, and always will be.

Someday Jesus will come to take us to be with Himself. Jesus gave this promise in John 14:1-3:

> Do not let your heart be troubled; believe in God, believe also in Me. In My Father's house are many dwelling places; if it were not so, I would have told you; for I go to prepare a place for you. If I go and prepare a place for you, I

will come again and receive you to Myself, that
where I am, there you may be also.

In these verses, three points are emphasized—a person,
a place, and a promise. The person is Jesus, the place is
heaven, and the promise is that He will come again someday to take His people there.

We Are Encouraged to Meet Together Regularly and Strengthen One Another

Hebrews 10:24-25 reminds us to "consider how to
stimulate one another to love and good deeds, not for-
saking our own assembling together, as is the habit of
some, but encouraging one another; and all the more
as you see the day drawing near." The writer of Hebrews
reminds us that as the days get darker and the time of
the Lord's coming draws near, we should be prompted
more than ever to gather together with God's people for
encouragement and strength. Don't get isolated from
other believers. We need each other. Far too many pro-
fessing Christians today are not vitally connected to a
local church. You need to allow God to use you to bring
encouragement to others in their time of need and let
others minister to you when you need to be uplifted. But
we can't do this effectively if we are not living out the life-
on-life contact God intended for us to experience in the
local church.

Find a local church that believes and teaches God's

Word and get involved there using the gifts and abilities God has given you to build up others and glorify God. And as you see the day of the Lord's coming draw nearer, stay committed, being available to support and help one another.

We Can Have an Eternal Perspective in a Shortsighted World

One of the advantages God's people have is that they can adopt a long-term perspective when it comes to daily circumstances and world events, as 2 Corinthians 4:16-18 reminds us:

> Therefore we do not lose heart, but though our outer man is decaying, yet our inner man is being renewed day by day. For momentary, light affliction is producing for us an eternal weight of glory far beyond all comparison, while we look not at the things which are seen, but at the things which are not seen; for the things which are seen are temporal, but the things which are not seen are eternal.

In a world that's dominated by the 24-hour news cycle of cable TV that brings us the very latest on all that's taking place, we can see the distant horizon and know where it's all headed. We can see beyond the temporal to the eternal and beyond what's seen to what's unseen.

We Can Live Pure Lives in Evil Days

The world exerts its strong pull on our lives, enticing us to live according to its values and mind-set. The Word of God, however, makes it clear that a proper understanding of Bible prophecy will inspire us to lives of holiness and purity. Peter drives this point home:

> The day of the Lord will come like a thief, in which the heavens will pass away with a roar and the elements will be destroyed with intense heat, and the earth and its works will be burned up. Since all these things are to be destroyed in this way, what sort of people ought you to be in holy conduct and godliness, looking for and hastening the coming of the day of God, because of which the heavens will be destroyed by burning, and the elements will melt with intense heat! But according to His promise we are looking for new heavens and a new earth, in which righteousness dwells. Therefore, beloved, since you look for these things, be diligent to be found by Him in peace, spotless and blameless (2 Peter 3:10-14).

Paul also encourages believers, "Live sensibly, righteously and godly in the present age, looking for the blessed hope and the appearing of the glory of our great God and Savior, Jesus Christ" (Titus 2:12-13).

Prophecy and purity are mentioned together in Romans 13:11-14:

> This is all the more urgent, for you know how late it is; time is running out. Wake up, for our salvation is nearer now than when we first believed. The night is almost gone; the day of salvation will soon be here. So remove your dark deeds like dirty clothes, and put on the shining armor of right living. Because we belong to the day, we must live decent lives for all to see. Don't participate in the darkness of wild parties and drunkenness, or in sexual promiscuity and immoral living, or in quarreling and jealously. Instead, clothe yourself with the presence of the Lord Jesus Christ. And don't let yourself think about ways to indulge your evil desires (NLT).

One final verse worth remembering is 1 John 3:2-3: "Beloved, now we are children of God, and it has not appeared as yet what we will be. We know that when He appears, we will be like Him, because we will see Him just as He is. And everyone who has this hope fixed on Him purifies himself, just as He is pure."

In light of what we know is coming, we should live our lives in a way that pleases God and reflects our understanding of the ultimate destiny of ourselves and this world. We should live for what lasts rather than spending our efforts pursuing empty, earthly pleasures.

We Are Motivated to Share God's Good News with Others

Knowing what's ahead for this world and for those who are outside of Christ should serve as a supreme stimulus for all who know Him to share the good news with others. The apostle Paul wrote his final inspired letter, known as 2 Timothy, from a Roman prison cell. The letter was directed to his colaborer Timothy. It's clear from the letter that Paul knew tumultuous times were ahead and that Timothy could be tempted to give up.

With that in mind, Paul makes this appeal to Timothy:

> I solemnly charge you in the presence of God and of Christ Jesus, who is to judge the living and the dead, and by His appearing and His kingdom: preach the word; be ready in season and out of season; reprove, rebuke, exhort, with great patience and instruction...But you, be sober in all things, endure hardship, do the work of an evangelist, fulfill your ministry (2 Timothy 4:1-2,5).

Paul knew that danger was on the horizon, but he looked far beyond the impending trouble to the time of Christ's coming and the final judgment. In light of that day, Paul urged Timothy and each of us to faithfully proclaim the good news as an evangelist (one who brings good news). All who know Christ should do everything we can to give as many people as possible the opportunity to hear the good news of forgiveness and eternal life through faith in Jesus.

We are Christ's ambassadors in a foreign land. It's up to us as God's people to spread the good news of salvation through Jesus Christ. "Therefore, we are ambassadors for Christ, as though God were making an appeal through us; we beg you on behalf of Christ, be reconciled to God" (2 Corinthians 5:20).

God's message about what is to come is not only to fill our heads but also to change our hearts. When the events outlined in this book are fulfilled (and they may be very soon), what difference should it make in your life today? The answer to that question could well decide your eternal destiny.

Appendixes

The Persia Prophecies

Winston Churchill once said, "The farther backward you can look, the farther forward you are likely to see." The same is true when it comes to understanding Bible prophecy. The past fulfillment of prophecy establishes the pattern for future fulfillment. With this maxim in mind, let's survey what Scripture says about Persia (Iran) in the past and how that affects what we see today.

The words *Persia, Persian,* and *Persians* occur a total of thirty-five times in the Old Testament. Thirty-four of these references clearly refer to the ancient Persian Empire and have, therefore, already been literally fulfilled. However, the reference to Persia in Ezckiel 38:5 is still future in our day and refers to the modern nation of Iran. The name was changed from Persia to Iran in 1935, and then to the Islamic Republic of Iran in 1979.

This book is primarily about current events in the Middle East and future prophecies regarding Iran and

Israel. But many people may not be aware that the Bible has accurately prophesied events about Israel and Iran (ancient Persia) that have already been fulfilled. Because other biblical prophecies about ancient Persia have been literally fulfilled, we can rest assured that when the time comes, the prophecy in Ezekiel 38 will be literally fulfilled as well.

THE CYRUS PROPHECY

The first specific Old Testament prophecy about Persia is found in the writing of the Hebrew prophet Isaiah, who wrote during the golden age of the Hebrew prophets in the eighth century BC. His prophecies are astounding in their detail. Writing in about 700 BC, he named the Medo-Persian King Cyrus by name about 100 years before he was born and almost 150 years before he rose to power.

Cyrus is a towering figure in Persian history. He led the ancient nation to great victories, territorial expansion, and astounding prosperity. Cyrus began his conquests in about 550 BC, enjoying unparalleled success, but his career culminated when he took the city of Babylon in October 539 BC as recorded in Daniel 5. Isaiah calls him by name and chronicles his reign in detail:

> "It is I who says of Cyrus, 'He is My shepherd!
> And he will perform all My desire.' And he

declares of Jerusalem, 'She will be built,' and
of the temple, 'Your foundation will be laid.'"
Thus says the LORD to Cyrus His anointed,
whom I have taken by the right hand to sub-
due nations before him and to loose the loins
of kings; to open doors before him so that gates
will not be shut (Isaiah 44:28–45:1).

If one accepts Isaiah's authorship of the book of Isaiah,
as I do, then there is no other way to understand these
words. Isaiah clearly proclaimed King Cyrus by name
about 100 years before he was born. It is accurate prophecies like this that set the Bible apart from any other book
that's ever been written.

Isaiah 41:2-4 and verse 25 clearly make reference to
Cyrus, but Isaiah 44:28 and 45:1 specifically name him.
Isaiah 45:2-6 goes on to predict the conquests of Cyrus
and his restoration of the Jewish people to their land. Isaiah 44:28 foretells his restoration of the Jews to their land
and their temple worship: "It is I who says of Cyrus, 'He
is My shepherd! And he will perform all My desire.' And
he declares of Jerusalem, 'She will be built,' and of the
temple, 'Your foundation will be laid.'" This was dramatically fulfilled in 2 Chronicles 36:22-23:

Now in the first year of Cyrus king of Persia—
in order to fulfill the word of the LORD by the
mouth of Jeremiah—the LORD stirred up the

spirit of Cyrus king of Persia, so that he sent a proclamation throughout his kingdom, and also put it in writing, saying, "Thus says Cyrus king of Persia, 'The LORD, the God of heaven, has given me all the kingdoms of the earth, and He has appointed me to build Him a house in Jerusalem, which is in Judah. Whoever there is among you of all His people, may the LORD his God be with him, and let him go up!'" (see also Ezra 1:1-11).

Liberal critics who deny the inspiration of the Bible and approach it with an antisupernatual bias reject any possibility of God foretelling the future. They contend that Isaiah was not written in the eighth century BC before Cyrus came to power, but by someone else later after Cyrus was already born and he had accomplished his exploits.[1] Alfred Martin, an Old Testament scholar, gets to the heart of the issue:

> This is actually the crux of the problem as far as the attitude of critics toward the Book of Isaiah is concerned...Here is Isaiah in the eighth century B.C. announcing Cyrus as the restorer of the people to Jerusalem, Cyrus who lived in the sixth century B.C....The whole point of the passage is that God, the omniscient God, is the One who announces events beforehand. That is the proof of His deity. The destructive critics

who say this passage must have been written in the sixth century by some otherwise unknown prophet in Babylon ("Deutero-Isaiah") are making the same stupid mistake that the idolaters of Isaiah's day were making. They are like the Sadducees of another time, to whom the Lord Jesus Christ said, "Ye do err, not knowing the scriptures, nor the power of God" (Matt. 22:29).[2]

It's incredible that critics who deny the authenticity of Isaiah totally miss the point. The Cyrus prophecies are found in Isaiah 41–46, a section of the Bible that is extolling God as the only One who can accurately foretell the future. The Cyrus prophecies are set forth by God as "Exhibit A" of His ability to predict events before they occur. In the surrounding context, notice how many times God drives home the point that only He can accurately forecast the future.

Isaiah 41:21-24

"Present your case," the LORD says. "Bring forward your strong arguments," the king of Jacob says. Let them bring forth and declare to us what is going to take place; as for the former events, declare what they were, that we may consider them and know their outcome. Or announce to us what is coming; declare the things that are going to come afterward, that we may know that you are gods; indeed, do good or evil, that we may anxiously look about us and fear together. Behold, you are of no account, and your work amounts to nothing; he who chooses you is an abomination.

Isaiah 42:9

Behold, the former things have come to pass, now I declare new things; before they spring forth I proclaim them to you.

Isaiah 45:21

Declare and set forth your case; indeed, let them consult together. Who has announced this from of old? Who has long since declared it? Is it not I, the LORD? And there is no other God besides Me, a righteous God and a Savior; there is none except Me.

Isaiah 46:9-10

Remember the former things long past, for I am God, and there is no other; I am God, and there is no one like Me, declaring the end from the beginning, and from ancient times things which have not been done, saying, "My purpose will be established, and I will accomplish all my good pleasure."

The very next words after Isaiah 46:9-10, where God proclaims that only He can tell the future, are a direct prophecy about Cyrus the Great: "Calling a bird of prey from the east, the man of My purpose from a far country. Truly I have spoken; truly I will bring it to pass. I have planned it, surely I will do it" (Isaiah 46:11).

God likens Cyrus to a bird of prey that He will summon from the east to accomplish His purposes.

Liberal critics would strip away the key prophecy in this section that God provides to prove that He is the only true God as He repeatedly affirms in Isaiah 41–46. Adopting their view would mean that God is no different from idols—the very point that Isaiah is disproving. Nevertheless, despite their unbelief, the Cyrus prophecy stands firm as the ultimate proof of the truth of these amazing claims and serves as the first great Old Testament prophecy about Persia.

DANIEL AND THE LATTER DAYS

The other main Old Testament predictions about Persia are found in the prophecies of Daniel. Three times Daniel predicted the rise of Persia on the heels of the Babylonian Empire.

Daniel 2: The Silver Kingdom

Daniel 2 records the dream of the Babylonian king Nebuchadnezzar and the interpretation of that dream by

Daniel. In his dream, Nebuchadnezzar saw a huge statue of a man consisting of four different materials. The four metals in the great statue represented four great empires that would appear successively on the world scene to rule over the civilized world of that day and on into the end times. With the 20/20 hindsight of history, we now know that these four empires were Babylon, Medo-Persia, Greece, and Rome. The feet and the ten toes of iron and clay point forward, even from our day, to a final, ten-king form of the Roman Empire. Daniel predicted the rise of the Persian Empire while Babylon was still ruling and accurately saw the future fall of Persia to Greece, which occurred 200 years after Daniel died. The transfer of power from Babylon to Persia occurred on October 12, 539 BC, and is recorded in dramatic fashion in Daniel 5.

Daniel 7: The Big Bear

Daniel 7 covers the same material in Daniel 2, yet with different imagery. Here the four empires are pictured not as metals but as monsters.

> In the first year of Belshazzar king of Babylon Daniel saw a dream and visions in his mind as he lay on his bed; then he wrote the dream down and related the following summary of it. Daniel said, "I was looking in my vision by night, and behold, the four winds of heaven

were stirring up the great sea. And four great beasts were coming up from the sea, different from one another. The first was like a lion and had the wings of an eagle. I kept looking until its wings were plucked, and it was lifted up from the ground and made to stand on two feet like a man; a human mind also was given to it. And behold, another beast, a second one, resembling a bear. And it was raised up on one side, and three ribs were in its mouth between its teeth; and thus they said to it, 'Arise, devour much meat!' After this I kept looking, and behold, another one, like a leopard, which had on its back four wings of a bird; the beast also had four heads, and dominion was given to it" (Daniel 7:1-6).

Babylon, the winged lion, is replaced by Persia, the bloodthirsty bear, which in turn is conquered by the Greek empire, pictured as a four-headed leopard with four wings. All this happened in history just as the Bible predicted.

Daniel 8: East Meets West

The final main Persian prophecy from Daniel was given in chapter 8, where the Persian Empire was pictured as a mighty two-horned ram that is gored and killed by a powerful goat with a large horn that symbolized the Greek Empire led by Alexander the Great. The imagery is confirmed in Daniel 8:20-21: "The ram which you saw with the two horns represents the kings of Media and Persia. And the shaggy goat represents the kingdom of Greece: and the large horn that is between his eyes is the first king." East met west, and the west won.

History in Advance

The ancient Persian Empire ruled the world for 200 years (539–331 BC) in power and human splendor— just as Daniel predicted when he spoke about the silver kingdom, the bloodthirsty bear, and the two-horned ram. But, in 331 BC, her splendor was ruined by the Greek Empire, which is represented by the bronze kingdom in Daniel 2, the four-headed leopard in Daniel 7, and the male goat in Daniel 8. The prophecies of Scripture concerning Persia were all fulfilled to a *T*.

After Persia's demise in the fourth century BC, she passed off the scene as a dominant power and eventually deteriorated into a second-rate nation with little power or prestige in the world. However, in the last 35 years, that situation has been dramatically reversed. Today, Iran is the major player in the Middle East. The rise of Iran is a key stage-setting event for the drama to take place during the end times. Iran must be a key player in the Middle East for the ancient prophecy of

Ezekiel 38–39 to be fulfilled. And we can be certain that the final prophecies regarding Iran in Ezekiel 38–39 will be fulfilled just as literally and specifically as the ones that have already come to pass as predicted by Isaiah and Daniel.

Is Syria About to Be Destroyed?

"There can be no peace without Syria."[1]

Henry Kissinger

Syria has dominated the news for several years since the days of the Arab Spring. A lot of attention has been given to the civil war that erupted in that country—a war that pits various rebel factions against the brutal regime of Bashar al-Assad. In an attempt to flee the fighting, millions of refugees have fled Syria into Europe and the surrounding nations.

The Assad family has ruled Syria with an iron fist for more than forty years. The family comes from "the Alawite mountains overlooking the Mediterranean which is a stronghold of the secretive sect with links to Shi'ite Islam."[2] This Alawite minority rules the Sunni majority in Syria; thus, the ingredients are present for long-standing grudges and the desire for payback. The Shiite

background of the Assad family has made them a natural ally of Iran and Iran's Lebanese proxy, Hezbollah, also
made up of Shiites. Syria has been a willing partner in
the Shiite crescent that Iran aspires to create to extend its
domination. Syria signed a mutual defense pact with Iran
in 2005 in which Syria agreed to allow the deployment of
Iranian weapons on its territory. Syria and Iran signed an
additional defense agreement in December 2009 aimed
to face "common enemies and challenges."[3] With the
outbreak of the civil war, Syria has become a satellite state
for Iran, giving Iran a staging ground on Israel's northern
border.

When the unrest erupted in Syria, Assad quickly
blamed "conspirators" for the protests. Many wondered
if the Assad regime would ultimately fall in the same way
Mubarek was ousted in Egypt and Gadhafi was overthrown and killed in Libya. As long as the military stands
with Assad and he continues to receive military support
from Russia and Iran, he and his cruel regime appear to
be very safe. Assad and his acolytes have shown themselves willing to use brutal means and bloody crackdowns
to stay in power, even to the point of unleashing chemical
weapons on their own people.

Another ally that has come to Syria's defense and
offered unwavering support is the Lebanese terrorist group and Iranian surrogate Hezbollah. The terrorist organization has a great deal to lose if Syrian president
Bashar al-Assad is deposed. It serves Hezbollah's purposes
to have a radical ally in Syria.

The unrest in Syria, added to all the other upheavals taking place in the Middle East, has left Israel on edge. Syria has been an entrenched enemy of Israel since the formation of the modern state. Israel and Syria have fought each other in three bloody wars: the War of Independence (1948), the Six-Day War (1967), and the Yom Kippur War (1973).

More recently, in September 2007, Israel destroyed Syria's Deir ez Zor nuclear plant in northern Syria, which heightened the already-tense standoff between the nations. A confidential report in 2011 by the International Atomic Energy Agency (IAEA), the U.N. nuclear watchdog, says the Deir ez Zor site in the desert was a covert nuclear plant designed to produce plutonium. The IAEA officially stated "that Syria was constructing a covert nuclear reactor, and we believe that reactor was designed to produce plutonium for possible use in nuclear weapons."[4] To complicate matters, Russia has stepped up and is considering how it can help Syria to build a nuclear reactor.

The new nuclear angle, along with the persistent upheaval in Syria, has added to Israel's angst. The fear of the unknown can be worse than the fear of the known, even if it's unsavory. Syria is a formidable military foe.

While considered inferior to Israel's military might, "the Assad regime fields armed forces totaling more than 380,000 men, with another 130,000 troops in reserve. Syria's arsenal includes approximately 3,700 tanks and some 510 combat aircraft."[5] If this military machine were to fall into even more radical, unstable hands, all bets would be off for Israel. The *Los Angeles Times* reported about growing Israeli fears concerning the unrest in Syria:

> As popular unrest threatens to topple another Arab neighbor, Israel finds itself again quietly rooting for the survival of an autocratic yet predictable regime, rather than face an untested new government in its place. Syrian President Bashar Assad's race to tamp down public unrest is stirring anxiety in Israel that is even higher than its hand-wringing over Egypt's recent regime change. Unlike Israel and Egypt, Israel and Syria have no peace agreement, and Syria, with a large arsenal of sophisticated weapons, is one of Israel's strongest enemies…Israel is worried about what might happen to Syria's arsenal, including Scud missiles, thousands of rockets capable of reaching all of Israel, chemical warheads, advanced surface-to-air systems and an aging air force. "You want to work with the devil you know," said Moshe Maoz, a former government advisor and Syria expert at Hebrew University's Harry S. Truman Institute for the Advancement of Peace.[6]

Israel now has another grave concern to add to its growing list of worries about its future as well as the future of the region. Assad, ISIS, Russia, Iran, and

Hezbollah are all in Syria. ISIS believes the final great battle of the ages will be waged in Dabiq, Syria, and that Jesus will return east of Damascus to bring judgment. For ISIS, Syria is the prize.

If Assad survives the attempts to depose him, which seems likely, Iran and Russia have an ongoing beachhead there, imperiling Israel. If Assad's regime were somehow to fall, whoever succeeds him would almost certainly be more radical and could push the already-dire situation over the brink, triggering an all-out conflagration. Or Syria could fracture at some point into tribal sects rife with instability. Any of these scenarios are possible, and any of them could lead down a path toward an Israeli preemptive strike against Syria.

Could it be that another nightmarish military conflict between Israel and Syria is just around the corner? Many believe this is where we're headed. They think this is exactly what the Bible predicts for Syria in the near future. This view is based on an ancient prophecy proclaimed by Isaiah.

Syria and Isaiah 17

One of the next key end-time events, according to many prophecy teachers, is the destruction of Damascus, the capital of Syria. This view is based on Isaiah 17:1-2, which says, "The oracle concerning Damascus. 'Behold, Damascus is about to be removed from being a city and will become a fallen ruin. The cities of Aroer are forsaken; they will be for flocks to lie down in, and there will be no one to frighten them.'"

Those who hold this view maintain that Damascus has never been removed from being a city, so if this prophecy is to be literally fulfilled it must occur in the future. Specifics about the destruction differ, but many believe that this prophecy predicts an Israeli nuclear attack on Damascus. It's also often alleged that the supernatural destruction of Damascus is an event that will occur before or right after the rapture of the church. Some believe it's an event that could happen any day. Here's a representative statement in support of this view:

> In the last days, the Bible tells us of a horrible series of events that will take place in the lands of Israel and Syria. One of these events is the disappearance of Damascus as one of the premiere cities in the world...In the very near future, Damascus will once again play a major role in human events. The prophet Isaiah provides us with God's commentary on a future conflict between Damascus and Israel, and in so doing, he reveals certain prophecies which have been partially fulfilled in the past. However, the ultimate fulfillment of Isaiah 17 remains in the future. The current existence of Damascus, which will one day cease to be a city, as well as the historical absence of the coalition of nations

prophesied to attack Israel and be destroyed by God, is proof that Isaiah 17 prophesies events yet future.[7]

When Isaiah 17 text is quoted, often only the first two verses are cited. Again, they read, "The oracle concerning Damascus. 'Behold, Damascus is about to be removed from being a city and will become a fallen ruin. The cities of Aroer are forsaken; they will be for flocks to lie down in, and there will be no one to frighten them.'"

Yet if one keeps reading it becomes apparent that whenever the demise of Damascus occurs, Israel will also suffer devastation. In Isaiah's day, Ephraim was the name for the northern kingdom of Israel. Notice that at the same time Damascus is destroyed, Israel is too:

"The fortified city will disappear from Ephraim [the name for the ten northern tribes of Israel], and sovereignty from Damascus and the remnant of Aram; they will be like the glory of the sons of Israel," declares the LORD of hosts. Now in that day the glory of Jacob will fade, and the fatness of his flesh will become lean. It will be even like the reaper gathering the standing grain, as his arm harvests the ears, or it will be like one gleaning ears of grain in the valley of Rephaim. Yet gleanings will be left in it like the shaking of an olive tree, two or three olives on the topmost bough, four or five on the branches

of a fruitful tree, declares the LORD, the God of
Israel. In that day man will have regard for his
Maker and his eyes will look to the Holy One
of Israel (Isaiah 17:3-7).

Many prophecy teachers cite Isaiah 17:1-2 as a future
prophecy of the doom of Damascus and Syria that will
pave the way for Israel to become a great and prosper-
ous nation, yet Isaiah 17:3-7 says that at the same time
Damascus suffers devastation, Israel will also fall. Some
try to argue that the reference to Ephraim is the Palestinian territory that will also suffer defeat at the same
time as Damascus, but that seems far-fetched to me. I've
heard others say that if Israel launches a nuclear strike
on Damascus, the fallout from that strike will be the cul-
prit that ends up crippling Israel, but this seems to be a
stretch.

I believe that it is much better to hold that Isaiah 17
was fulfilled in the eighth century BC when both Damascus, the capital of Syria (732 BC), and Samaria, the capital of Israel a decade later (722 BC), were hammered by
the Assyrians. In those Assyrian conquests, it's very clear
that both Damascus and Samaria were destroyed, just as
Isaiah 17 predicts. According to history, Tiglath-pileser
III (745-727 BC) pushed vigorously to the west, and in
734 the Assyrians advanced and laid siege to Damascus,
which fell two years later in 732. Rezin, the Syrian mon-
arch, was executed, his kingdom was overthrown, and
the city suffered the fate which a few years later befell

Samaria. For Isaiah 17 to have been fulfilled in the eighth century BC is further supported by the final three verses of the chapter. Isaiah 17:12-14 says,

> Alas, the uproar of many peoples who roar like the roaring of the seas, and the rumbling of nations who rush on like the rumbling of mighty waters! The nations rumble on like the rumbling of many waters, but He will rebuke them and they will flee far away, and be chased like chaff in the mountains before the wind, or like whirling dust before a gale. At evening time, behold, there is terror! Before morning they are no more. Such will be the portion of those who plunder us and the lot of those who pillage us.

Some try to see this as a future reference to Israel gaining supremacy over its enemies in the end times, but this is a historical reference to God's destruction of the Assyrian army under Sennacherib in 701 BC, when the latter led a military campaign against Judah and Hezekiah the king. The Assyrians got their just desserts when they were destroyed by God. Isaiah 17:14 vividly refers to this: "At evening time, behold, there is terror! Before morning they are no more." Isaiah 37:37-38 records the fulfillment of this when 185,000 Assyrians fell in one night under the hand of divine judgment.

Jeremiah 49:23-27 is another biblical prophecy describing the destruction of Damascus. The destruction

here refers to what occurred in 605 BC, when Nebuchadnezzar, king of Babylon, swept through the ancient Near
East wreaking havoc on nation after nation. Nebuchadnezzar is mentioned several times in this section of Jeremiah, confirming that this is the time period involved
(46:2,13,26; 49:28).

But what about Isaiah's statement in 17:1, "Behold,
Damascus is about to be removed from being a city and
will become a fallen ruin"? The King James Version of
17:1 says, "The burden of Damascus. Behold, Damascus
is taken away from being a city, and it shall be a ruinous
heap." The ESV reads, "An oracle concerning Damascus.
Behold, Damascus will cease to be a city and will become
a heap of ruins." The NIV says, "A prophecy against
Damascus: See, Damascus will no longer be a city but
will become a heap of ruins."

Proponents of the end-time destruction of Damascus
viewpoint will ask, "When was this ever fulfilled literally
in the past?" To answer this question, we have to carefully
note what this text *does* and *does not* say. It does say that
Damascus will be destroyed and made a heap of ruins
and will be removed from being a city. That occurred literally in 732 BC when Damascus was destroyed by the
Assyrians under Tiglath-pileser. The text does not say that
Damascus would be removed "forever" from being a city.
It simply says that Damascus will be "removed" or "taken
away" from being a city. Isaiah 17 is a prophecy of a temporary desolation that happened to many nations in the

ancient Near East when they were destroyed by invading armies. Nowhere does Isaiah say that the city would never be rebuilt or inhabited again. I believe that Isaiah 17 was fulfilled in the ancient past, and so I don't see events today as portending its imminent fulfillment.

What Is Syria's Future?

Having made my view of Isaiah 17 clear, I do believe that events today in Syria point toward the fulfillment of key biblical prophecies. As the fuse on the powder keg that is the Middle East continues to burn, the stage is being set for the Middle East peace treaty prophesied in Daniel 9:27. The only solution to the Middle East quagmire, short of all-out conflagration, is some kind of regional, comprehensive peace agreement. In the current Middle East environment, with Syria as a key player, it makes sense that Syria would be part of any such peace agreement. After all, Henry Kissinger did say, "There can be no peace [in the Middle East] without Syria."

The chaos in Syria has also created a vacuum for Russia and Iran to fill. Their presence in Syria on Israel's northern border foreshadows the future invasion of Israel by these nations and their allies.

The futures of many nations are predicted in Scripture, as we have seen in Ezekiel 38–39, but the specific future of many other nations is not given. If Isaiah 17 and Jeremiah are not interpreted as end-time prophecies about Syria's destruction, then one is hard-pressed to find another particular prophecy that addresses its future in any detail.[8]

Yet we can rest assured that Syria will have its day of judgment—just like all other nations who come against Israel and the Lord.

America in Prophecy

(Dr. John F. Walvoord)

In our current age, we often fail to keep in touch with the past. Great teachers are too quickly forgotten. One of my teachers was Dr. John F. Walvoord, who served as president of Dallas Theological Seminary for 35 years. I've included this excerpt from his 1967 work *The Nations in Prophecy* so you can learn from his wise words, which still ring true today:

"AMERICA IN PROPHECY," BY DR. JOHN F. WALVOORD

One of the natural questions facing the world, but especially citizens of the United States of America, is the place of the United States in the unfulfilled prophetic program. In the last 50 years, the United States of America has become one of the most powerful and influential nations of all history. What does the Bible contribute to the question of the future of the United States?

In keeping with the principle that prophecy is primarily concerned with the Holy Land and its immediate neighbors, it is not surprising that geographic areas remote from this center of biblical interest should not figure largely in prophecy and may not be mentioned at all. No specific mention of the United States or any other country in North or South America can be found in the Bible. None of the rather obscure references to distant lands can be taken specifically as a reference to the United States. Any final answer to the question is therefore an impossibility, but nevertheless some conclusions of a general character can be reached.

The World Situation in the End Times

As previous study of prophecy has indicated, the Scriptures provide an outline of major events in the period beginning with the rapture of the church and ending with the second coming of Christ to establish His kingdom. Immediately after the rapture, there will be a period of preparation in which the ten-nation confederacy in the Mediterranean will emerge and the little horn of Daniel 7 will be revealed as its eventual dictator. At the same time, there will be the emergence of a world church as suggested in Revelation 17.

At the conclusion of this period of preparation, the head of the Mediterranean confederacy, who will be the Roman "prince that shall come," will make a covenant with Israel (Daniel 9:27), which will introduce the second phase of the period, namely, a period of protection and peace for Israel. After enduring for three-and-a-half years or one-half of the projected seven-year period contemplated in the covenant, the Roman ruler will take the role of world dictator, assume the prerogatives of deity, and begin the great Tribulation with its corresponding period of persecution for Israel and the emergence of a world religion with the world ruler as its deity. This third period will be climaxed by the second coming of Christ to the earth and its attending judgments.

The Relation of the United States to These World Events

Although the Scriptures do not give any clear word concerning the role of the United States in relationship to the revived Roman Empire and the later development of the world empire, it is probable that the United States will be in some form of alliance with the Roman ruler. Most citizens of the United States of America have come from Europe and their sympathies would be more naturally with a European alliance than with Russia or countries in Eastern Asia. It may even be that the United States will provide large support for the Mediterranean confederacy, as it seems to be in opposition to Russia, Eastern Asia, and Africa. Actually, a balance of power in the world may exist at that time not too dissimilar to the present world situation—namely, that Europe and the Mediterranean area will be in alliance with America in opposition to Russia, Eastern Asia, and Africa. Based on geographic, religious, and economic factors such an alliance of powers seems a natural sequence of present situations in the world.

If the end-time events include a destruction of Russia and her allies prior to the final period of the great Tribulation, this may trigger an unbalance in the world situation that will permit the Roman ruler to become a world ruler. In this event, it should be clear that the United States will be in a subordinate role and no longer the great international power that it is today.

It has been suggested by some that the total absence of Scriptural comment on the United States of America in the end times is evidence that the United States previously has been destroyed by an atomic war or some other catastrophic means and therefore no longer is a voice in international affairs. Such a solution, however, overlooks the fact that not only the United States but all of the Americas are omitted from prophecy, and the same is true of Australia. The fact is there are few references to any country at some distance from the Holy Land. The view, therefore, would be preferable that while the United States is in existence and possibly a power to be reckoned with in the rapidly moving events that characterize the end of the age, world political power will be centered in the Mediterranean area, and necessarily the United States will play a subordinate role.

History has many records of great nations that have risen to unusual power and influence, only to decline

because of internal corruption or international compli-
cations. It may well be that the United States of America
is today at the zenith of its power much as Babylon was
in the sixth century BC prior to its sudden downfall at
the hands of the Medes and the Persians (Daniel 5). Any
realistic survey of moral conditions in the world today
would justify a judgment of God on any nation, including that of the United States. The longsuffering God has
offered unusual benefits to the United States, both in a
material and religious way, but they have been used with
such profligacy that ultimate divine judgment may be
expected. The question no longer is whether America
deserves judgment, but rather why divine judgment has
been so long withheld from a nation which has enjoyed
so much of God's bounty.

A partial answer may be found in the fact that the
United States of America in spite of its failures has nevertheless been a source of major Christian testimony in
the world and has done more to promote the missionary
cause in terms of money and men than any other nation.
Although the United States numbers only five per cent of
the total world population, in the last century probably
more than fifty per cent of the missionaries and money
spent has come from America. In view of the fact that
it is God's major purpose in this present age to call out
Jew and Gentile to faith in Christ and to have the Gospel preached in all nations, the prosperity which has been
true of America has made possible this end and may have
been permitted by God to accomplish His holy purposes.

Another important reason for delay in divine judgment upon America is the Abrahamic promise concerning his seed, "I will bless them that bless thee, and curse him that curseth thee" (Genesis 12:3). The United States for the most part has been kind to the Jew. Here the seed of Abraham has had religious freedom and opportunity to make wealth. Judgment on other nations has frequently been preceded by persecution of the Jew. So far in the United States the Jew has had equal treatment.

It is evident, however, that if Christ came for His church and all true Christians were caught out of this world, America then would be reduced to the same situation as other countries. The true church will be gone, and Israel may be persecuted. The drastically changed situation would no longer call for material or political blessing upon the United States. It would therefore follow that with the removal of the principal cause for withholding judgment, namely, the promotion of the missionary cause and befriending the wandering Jew, reason would no longer exist for maintaining America in its present standard of power politically and economically. It may well be that the United States, like Babylon of old, will lose its place of leadership in the world, and this will be a major cause in the shift of power to the Mediterranean scene.

Conclusion

Although conclusions concerning the role of America in prophecy in the end time are necessarily tentative, the

Scriptural evidence is sufficient to conclude that America in that day will not be a major power and apparently does not figure largely in either the political, economic, or religious aspects of the world. America may well be at its zenith today both in power, influence, and opportunity. In view of the imminent return of the Lord, the time is short and the cause of evangelism is urgent. If prophecy has any one message as bearing on our times, it is that time and opportunity are short, and impending world conditions soon may close the door for further witness in many areas. What is true of America is true for the evangelical church throughout the world, and prophecy in general serves to emphasize the importance of the present task of bearing witness to the Gospel, beginning at Jerusalem and to the uttermost parts of the world.

The destiny of nations is in the hands of the omnipotent God. History is moving inexorably to its prophesied consummation. The divine program in all its detail will be fulfilled. The Son of God will reign in Zion. The nations will bow at His feet. Ultimately the present earth will be replaced with a new heaven and a new earth in which the New Jerusalem will be the home of the redeemed of all ages. All nations will continue throughout eternity to worship and adore the infinite Triune God whose majesty, wisdom, and power will be unquestioned. In that eternal day, God's love and grace will be supremely revealed in those among all nations who are redeemed by the blood of the Lamb.

Ezekiel 38–39

EZEKIEL 38: And the word of the LORD came to me saying, "Son of man, set your face toward Gog of the land of Magog, the prince of Rosh, Meshech and Tubal, and prophesy against him and say, 'Thus says the Lord GOD, "Behold, I am against you, O Gog, prince of Rosh, Meshech and Tubal. I will turn you about and put hooks into your jaws, and I will bring you out, and all your army, horses and horsemen, all of them splendidly attired, a great company with buckler and shield, all of them wielding swords; Persia, Ethiopia and Put with them, all of them with shield and helmet; Gomer with all its troops; Beth-togarmah from the remote parts of the north with all its troops—many peoples with you.

"Be prepared, and prepare yourself, you and all your companies that are assembled about you, and be a guard for them. After many days you will be summoned; in the latter years you will come into the land that is restored from the sword, whose inhabitants have been gathered from many nations to the mountains of Israel which had been a continual waste; but its people were brought out from the nations, and they are living securely, all of them. You will go up, you will come like a storm; you will be like a cloud covering the land, you and all your troops, and many peoples with you."

'Thus says the Lord GOD, "It will come about on that day, that thoughts will come into your mind and you will devise an evil plan, and you will say, 'I will go up against the land of unwalled villages. I will go against those who are at rest, that live securely, all of them living without walls and having no bars or gates, to capture spoil and to seize plunder, to turn your hand against the waste places which are now inhabited, and against the people who are gathered from the nations, who have acquired cattle and goods, who live at the center of the world.' Sheba and Dedan and the merchants of Tarshish with all its villages will say to you, 'Have you come to capture spoil? Have you assembled your company to seize plunder, to carry away silver and gold, to take away cattle and goods, to capture great spoil?'"'

"Therefore prophesy, son of man, and say to Gog, 'Thus says the Lord GOD, "On that day when My people Israel are living securely, will you not know it? You will come from your place out of the remote parts of the north, you and many peoples with you, all of them riding on horses, a great assembly and a mighty army; and you will come up against My people Israel like a cloud to cover the land. It shall come about in the last days that I will bring you against My land, so that the nations may know Me when I am sanctified through you before their eyes, O Gog."

'Thus says the Lord GOD, "Are you the one of whom I spoke in former days through My servants the prophets of Israel, who prophesied in those days for many years that I would bring you against them? It will come about on that day, when Gog comes against the land of Israel," declares the Lord GOD, "that My fury will mount up in My anger. In My zeal and in My blazing wrath I declare that on that day there will surely be a great earthquake in the land of Israel. The fish of the sea, the birds of the heavens, the beasts of the field, all the creeping things that creep on the earth, and all the men who are on the face of the earth will shake at My presence; the mountains also will be thrown down, the steep pathways will collapse and every wall will fall to the ground. I will call for a sword against him on all My mountains," declares the Lord GOD.

"Every man's sword will be against his brother. With pestilence and with blood I will enter into judgment with him; and I will rain on him and on his troops, and on the many peoples who are with him, a torrential rain, with hailstones, fire and brimstone. I will magnify Myself, sanctify Myself, and make Myself known in the sight of many nations; and they will know that I am the LORD.'"

EZEKIEL 39: "And you, son of man, prophesy against Gog and say, 'Thus says the Lord GOD, "Behold, I am against you, O Gog, prince of Rosh, Meshech and Tubal; and I will turn you around, drive you on, take you up from the remotest parts of the north and bring you against the mountains of Israel. I will strike your bow from your left hand and dash down your arrows from your right hand. You will fall on the mountains of Israel, you and all your troops and the peoples who are with you; I will give you as food to every kind of predatory bird and beast of the field. You will fall on the open field; for it is I who have spoken," declares the Lord GOD. "And I will send fire upon Magog and those who inhabit the coastlands in safety; and they will know that I am the LORD.

"My holy name I will make known in the midst of My people Israel; and I will not let My holy name be profaned anymore. And the nations will know that I am the LORD, the Holy One in Israel. Behold, it is coming and it shall be done," declares the Lord GOD. "That is the day of which I have spoken.

"Then those who inhabit the cities of Israel will go out and make fires with the weapons and burn them, both shields and bucklers, bows and arrows, war clubs and spears, and for seven years they will make fires of them. They will not take wood from the field or gather firewood from the forests, for they will make fires with the weapons; and they will take the spoil of those who despoiled them and seize the plunder of those who plundered them," declares the Lord GOD.

"On that day I will give Gog a burial ground there in Israel, the valley of those who pass by east of the sea, and it will block off those who would pass by. So they will bury Gog there with all his horde, and they will call it the valley of Hamon-gog. For seven months the house of Israel will be burying them in order to cleanse the land. Even all the people of the land will bury them; and it will be to their renown on the day that I glorify Myself," declares the Lord GOD. "They will set apart men who will constantly pass through the land, burying those who were passing through, even those left on the surface of the ground, in order to cleanse it. At the end of seven months they will make a search. As those who pass through the land pass through and anyone sees a man's bone, then he will set up a marker by it until the buriers have buried it in the valley of Hamon-gog. And even the name of the city will be Hamonah. So they will cleanse the land.'"

"As for you, son of man, thus says the Lord GOD, 'Speak to every kind of bird and to every beast of the field, "Assemble and come, gather from every side to My sacrifice which I am going to sacrifice for you, as a great sacrifice on the mountains of Israel, that you may eat flesh and drink blood. You will eat the flesh of mighty men and drink the blood of the princes of the earth, as though they were rams, lambs, goats and bulls, all of them fatlings of Bashan. So you will eat fat until you are glutted, and drink blood until you are drunk, from My sacrifice which I have sacrificed for you. You will be glutted at My table with horses and charioteers, with mighty men and all the men of war," declares the Lord GOD.

"And I will set My glory among the nations; and all

the nations will see My judgment which I have executed and My hand which I have laid on them. And the house of Israel will know that I am the LORD their God from that day onward. The nations will know that the house of Israel went into exile for their iniquity because they acted treacherously against Me, and I hid My face from them; so I gave them into the hand of their adversaries, and all of them fell by the sword. According to their uncleanness and according to their transgressions I dealt with them, and I hid My face from them.""'"

Therefore thus says the Lord GOD, "Now I will restore the fortunes of Jacob and have mercy on the whole house of Israel; and I will be jealous for My holy name. They will forget their disgrace and all their treachery which they perpetrated against Me, when they live securely on their own land with no one to make them afraid. When I bring them back from the peoples and gather them from the lands of their enemies, then I shall be sanctified through them in the sight of the many nations. Then they will know that I am the LORD their God because I made them go into exile among the nations, and then gathered them again to their own land; and I will leave none of them there any longer. I will not hide My face from them any longer, for I will have poured out My Spirit on the house of Israel," declares the Lord GOD.

NOTES

Chapter 1—Middle East Meltdown

1. Billy Graham, *World Aflame* (New York: Doubleday, 1965), 1.

2. "Hagel: I think we are seeing a new world order," *World Bulletin*, November 26, 2014, http://www.worldbulletin.net/news/149262/hagel-i-think-we-are-seeing-a-new-world-order.

3. Mina Al-Oraibi, "How ISIS' Attacks Harm the Middle East," *U.S. News and World Report*, November 23, 2015, http://www.usnews.com/news/articles/2015/11/23/how-isis-attacks-harm-the-middle-east.

4. Joel Rosenberg, "Apocalyptic Islam," November 5, 2015, http://prophecyupdate.blogspot.com/2015/11/apocalyptic-islam-by-joel-rosenberg.html.

5. Tim Lister, "What Does ISIS Really Want?" CNN, December 11, 2015, http://www.cnn.com/2015/12/11/middleeast/isis-syria-iraq-caliphate/index.html.

6. Lister, "What Does ISIS Really Want?"

7. Roi Kais, "ISIS leader to Israel: Palestine will be your graveyard," *Ynet news*, December 26, 2015, http://www.ynetnews.com/articles/0,7340,L-4744424,00.html.

8. John F. Walvoord, *Armageddon, Oil and the Middle East Crisis: What the Bible Says About the Future of the Middle East and the End of Western Civilization*, rev. ed. (Grand Rapids: Zondervan, 1990), 27.

Chapter 2—MetastISIS

1. Robert Spencer, *The Complete Infidel's Guide to ISIS* (Washington, D.C.: Regnery Publishing, 2015), xxi-xxii, 283.

2. Evan Perez, "U.S. facing 'unprecedented threat environment' in wake

of ISIS' rise," CNN, December 23, 2015, http://www.cnn.com/
2015/12/23/politics/isis-terrorism-us-fbi-prosecutions/index.html.

3. D.C. McAlister, "ISIS Celebrates San Bernardino Shooting," *The Federalist*, December 3, 2015, http://thefederalist.com/2015/12/03/
isis-celebrates-san-bernardino-shooting.

4. Evan Perez, "U.S. facing 'unprecedented threat environment' in wake of ISIS's rise," December 25, 2015, http://fox13now.com/2015/12/25/
u-s-facing-unprecedented-threat-environment-in-wake-of-isiss-rise/.

5. Spencer, *The Complete Infidel's Guide to ISIS*, 104.

6. Spencer, *The Complete Infidel's Guide to ISIS*.

7. Jay Akbar and Isabel Hunter, "Beheadings, crucifixions and bombs falling from the sky: Life inside the burned out 'ghost town' of ISIS capital Raqqa where 'prisoners' live amongst the rubble with no electricity or hot water," *Daily Mail*, December 15, 2015, http://www
.dailymail.co.uk/news/article-3359510/Inside-ISIS-capital-Raqqa
-beheadings-crucifixions-bombs-sky.html.

8. William McCants, *The ISIS Apocalypse* (New York: St. Martin's Press, 2015), 6.

9. Spencer, *The Complete Infidel's Guide to ISIS*, 67.

10. Erika Solomon and Sam Jones, "Isis Inc: From loot to oil, taxes keep jihadi economy churning," *Financial Times*, December 14, 2015, http://finance.yahoo.com/news/isis-inc-loot-oil-taxes-170252934
.html.

11. Spencer, *The Complete Infidel's Guide to ISIS*, 106.

12. Spencer, *The Complete Infidel's Guide to ISIS*.

13. Solomon and Jones, "Isis Inc: From loot to oil, taxes keep jihadi economy churning."

14. Charles H. Dyer and Mark Tobey, *The ISIS Crisis* (Chicago: Moody Publishers, 2015).

15. Eric McClam, "Tracing the Rise of ISIS into a Menace of Terror," NBC News, September 29, 2014, www.nbcnews.com/storyline/
isis-terror/tracing-rise-isis-menace.

Chapter 3—ISIS Apocalypse

1. Graeme Wood, "What ISIS Really Wants," *The Atlantic*, March 2015, http://www.theatlantic.com/magazine/archive/2015/03/what-isis-really-wants/384980/.

2. Tim Lister, "What Does ISIS Really Want?" CNN, December 11, 2015, http://www.cnn.com/2015/12/11/middlecast/isis-syria-iraq-caliphate/index.html.

3. "Tony Abbott intensifies rhetoric about Isis, calling it an 'apocalyptic death cult,'" http://www.theguardian.com/world/2014/sep/30/tony-abbott-intensifies-rhetoric-about-isis-calling-it-an-apocalyptic-death-cult.

4. William McCants, *The ISIS Apocalypse* (New York: St. Martin's Press, 2015), 15.

5. "Inside the Islamic State's Apocalyptic Beliefs," an interview with expert Will McCants. Nick Robins-Early, *The Huffington Post*, September 26, 2015.

6. Wood, "What ISIS Really Wants."

7. Wood, "What ISIS Really Wants."

8. Cathy Burke, "ISIS Wants Armageddon-Style Battle in Syria," *Newsmax*, November 17, 2015, http://www.newsmax.com/Headline/ISIS-armageddon-style-battle-syria/2015/11/17/id/702480/.

9. Robert Spencer, *The Complete Infidel's Guide to ISIS* (Washington D.C.: Regnery Publishing, 2015), 71.

10. Joel Rosenberg, "Apocalyptic Islam," November 5, 2015, http://prophecyupdate.blogspot.com/2015/11/apocalyptic-islam-by-joel-rosenberg.html.

11. "Who Is Imam al-Mahdi?" www.islamicweb.com/history/mahdi.htm7.

12. Adam Eliyahu Berkowitz, "With ISIS Poised for War, Is the West Playing into Their Plans for Armageddon?" December 31, 2015, http://www.breakingisraelnews.com/57389/o0bama-playing-into-hands-isis-end-of-days-prophecies-terror-watch/#Tq3UwKme5vJ2J8DG.97.

13. McCants, *The ISIS Apocalypse*, 27.

14. Tim LaHaye, *Jesus: Why the World Is Still Fascinated by Him* (Colorado Springs, CO: David C. Cook, 2009), 43.

15. Lister, "What Does ISIS Really Want?"

Chapter 4—The Ezekiel Prophecy

1. John Mark Ruthven, *The Prophecy That Is Shaping History* (Fairfax, VA: Xulon Press, 2003), i.

2. Thomas Ice, "Ezekiel 38 and 39: Part II," www.pre-trib.org/data/pdf/Ice-(Part2)Ezekiel38&39.pdf, accessed July 30, 2012.

3. Charles Dyer and Mark Tobey, *ISIS Crisis* (Chicago: Moody Publishers, 2015), 99.

4. Josephus, *Antiquities* 1.6.1.

5. The Hebrew scholar Heinrich Friedrich Wilhelm Gesenius identified Rosh as Russia. See Heinrich Friedrich Wilhelm Gesenius, *Gesenius' Hebrew-Chaldee Lexicon to the Old Testament* (Grand Rapids: Eerdmans, 1949), 752. For an excellent presentation of the grammatical and philological support for taking Rosh as a place name, see James D. Price, "Rosh: An Ancient Land Known to Ezekiel," *Grace Theological Journal* 6 (1985): 67-89; Clyde E. Billington, Jr., "The Rosh People in History and Prophecy (Part One)," *Michigan Theological Journal* 3 (1992): 55-64; Clyde E. Billington Jr., "The Rosh People in History and Prophecy (Part Two)" *Michigan Theological Journal* 3 (1992): 143-174; Clyde E. Billington Jr., "The Rosh People in History and Prophecy (Part Three)," *Michigan Theological Journal* 4 (1993): 39-62; Jon Mark Ruthven and Ihab Griess, *The Prophecy That Is Shaping History: New Research on Ezekiel's Vision of the End* (Longwood, FL: Xulon Press, 2003), 61-62.

6. General Jerry Boykin, Epicenter Conference, San Diego, April 4, 2009.

7. Thomas Ice, "The Battle between Russia, Iran and Israel," http://practicalspiritualwarfare.com/end-times-8.html.

8. Melik Kaylan, "Russia's Stake in Syria and Iran," March 18, 2012, WSJ.com, http://online.wsj.com/article/SB10001424052702304450004577277820529873332.html, accessed July 30, 2012.

9. "Russia denies war games report," June 19, 2012, http://www.upi.com/Top_News/World-News/2012/06/19/Iran-Russia-China-Syria-to

-hold-drill/UPI-93751340106919/#ixzz1yFVH50Xn, accessed July 30, 2012.

10. "Bashir: Sharia law will be strengthened if South Sudan votes to secede," *The Christian Science Monitor*, http://www.csmonitor.com/World/Africa/Africa-Monitor/2010/1223/Bashir-Sharia-law-will-be, accessed July 30, 2012.

11. Maggie Michael, "Freed of Gadhafi, Libya's Instability Only Deepens," *The Daily Oklahoman*, March 4, 2012, 13A.

12. Josephus, *Antiquities* 1.6.1. Yamauchi provides a thorough description of the ancient Scythians. See Edwin M. Yamauchi, *Foes from the Northern Frontier* (Grand Rapids: Baker Book House, 1992), 64-109.

13. Arnold Fruchtenbaum, *The Footsteps of the Messiah: A Study of the Sequence of Prophetic Events*, rev. ed. (Tustin, CA: Ariel Ministries, 2003), 111-12.

14. Heinrich Friedrich Wilhelm Gesenius, *Gesenius' Hebrew-Chaldee Lexicon of the Old Testament* (Grand Rapids: Baker, 1979), 875.

15. Fruchtenbaum, *The Footsteps of the Messiah: A Study of the Sequence of Prophetic Events*, 111.

16. Fruchtenbaum, *The Footsteps of the Messiah: A Study of the Sequence of Prophetic Events*, 112.

Chapter 5—Showdown in the Middle East: Iran and Israel

1. Eliott C. McLaughlin, "Iran's supreme leader: There will be no such thing as Israel in 25 years," CNN.com, September 11, 2015, http://www.cnn.com/2015/09/10/middleeast/iran-khamenei israel-will-not-exist-25-years/.

2. Steven Horowitz, "Israel and the Russian 'Spring,'" *The Times of Israel*, October 16, 2015, http://blogs.timesofisrael.com/israel-and-the-russian-spring/.

3. "Iran profile—timeline," BBC News, July 14, 2015, http://www.bbc.com/news/world-middle-east-14542438.

4. Yaakov Katz and Yoaz Hendel, *Israel vs. Iran: The Shadow War* (Washington, DC: Potomac Books, 2012), 9.

5. "Iran has more missiles than it can hide," *Yahoo News*, January 1, 2016,

http://news.yahoo.com/iran-more-missiles-hide-general-140851452
.html.

6. Katz and Hendel, *Israel vs. Iran: The Shadow War*, 167-68.

7. Matthew Gutman, "Israeli pilot recalls smashing a rival's nuclear ambitions," www.usatoday.com/news/world/2006-03-07-israel-osiraq_x
.htm, accessed July 26, 2012.

8. Jeffrey Goldberg, "Israelis Grow Confident Strike on Iran's Nukes Can Work," *Bloomberg*, March 19, 2012, http://www.bloomberg.com/
news/2012-03-19/israelis-grow-confident-strike-on-iran-s-nukes-can
-work.html, accessed July 26, 2012.

9. Ronen Bergman, "Will Israel Attack Iran?" *The New York Times*,
January 25, 2012, http://www.nytimes.com/2012/01/29/magazine/will
-israel-attack-iran.html?_r=1&pagewanted=all, accessed July 26, 2012.

10. Elizabeth Bumiller, "Iran Raid Seen as Huge Task for Israeli Jets," *The New York Times*, February 19, 2012.

11. D.B. Grady, "If Israel Bombs Iran: Forecasting the Next 24 Hours,"
The Week, March 19, 2012, http://theweek.com/bullpen/column/
225737/if-israel-bombs-iran-forecasting-the-next-24-hours, accessed
July 26, 2012.

12. "Khamenei: Israel is a cancerous tumor," *Jerusalem World News*, February 3, 2011, http://jerusalemworldnews.com/2012/02/03/
khamenei-israel-is-a-cancerous-tumor.

13. Katz and Hendel, *Israel vs. Iran: The Shadow War*, 114.

14. "Iranian Details Plans to Annihilate Israel," *Israel My Glory*, May–June 2012, 35.

15. Julian Borger, "Iran Warns Israel of 'Lightning' Reply to Any Attack,"
The Guardian, June 3, 2012, http://www.guardian.co.uk/world/2012/
jun/03/iran-supreme-leader-israel-attack?newsfeed=true, accessed July
26, 2012.

16. Reza Kahlili, "Iran Warns World of Coming Great Event,"
WND.com, February 2, 2012, http://www.wnd.com/2012/02/
iran-warns-world-of-coming-great-event/.

17. Max Fisher, "Fear Itself: Americans Believe Iran Threat on Par with
1980s Soviet Union," *The Atlantic*, April 19, 2012, http://www.the
atlantic.com/international/archive/2012/04/fear-itself-americans

-believe-iran-threat-on-par-with-1980s-soviet-union/256135, accessed July 26, 2012.

18. Fisher, "Fear Itself: Americans Believe Iran Threat on Par with 1980s Soviet Union."

19. Fisher, "Fear Itself: Americans Believe Iran Threat on Par with 1980s Soviet Union."

20. Katz and Hendel, *Israel vs. Iran: The Shadow War*, 167-87.

21. George Jahn, "Iran nuke work at bunker is confirmed," January 10, 2012, http://www.timesargus.com/article/20120110/NEWS/701109997/0/OPINION01.

22. Rebecca Ann Stoil, "Barak: Qom Plant Immune to Regular Strike," *Jerusalem Post*, December 28, 2009.

23. "Israel ambassador keeps door open to Iran strike," CBS News, March 15, 2012, http://www.cbsnews.com/8301-505263_162-57397940/israel-ambassador-keeps-door-open-to-iran-strike, accessed July 26, 2012.

24. "Exclusive: Cornered but unbound by nuclear pact, Israel reconsiders military action against Iran," *The Jerusalem Post*, January 4, 2016, http://www.jpost.com/International/Exclusive-Cornered-but-unbound-by-nuclear-pact-Israel-reconsiders-military-action-against-Iran-382541.

25. David Barnhart, *Living in the Times of the Signs* (Maitland, FL: Xulon Press, 2007), 215.

26. Fred Kaplan, "October Surprise: Why Israel May Feel Pressure to Attack Iran Before the U.S. Presidential Election," April 12, 2012, http://www.slate.com/articles/news_and_politics/war_stories/2012/04/nuclear_iran_why_i, accessed July 26, 2012.

27. This story from Barnhouse is related by James Montgomery Boice, *The Last and Future World* (Grand Rapids: Zondervan Publishing House, 1974), 49-50.

Chapter 6—Show Me the Mahdi

1. Mortimer B. Zuckerman, "Moscow's Mad Gamble," *U.S. News and World Report*, January 30, 2006, Internet edition.

2. Joel C. Rosenberg, "Iranian Defense Minister: War with Israel Means

Twelfth Imam Is Coming," September 21, 2012, http://flashtrafficblog
.wordpress.com/2012/09/21/iranian-defense-minister-war-with-
israel-means-twelfth-imam-is-coming/.

3. Reza Kahlili, "Iran committed to 'full annihilation of Israel,' says top
   Iranian military commander," *The Daily Caller*, May 20, 2012, http://
   news.yahoo.com/iran-committed-full annihilation-israel-says-top
   -iranian033409439.html.

4. Thomas Erdbrink, "Iran's Vice President Makes Anti-Semitic Speech at
   Conference," *The New York Times,* June 26, 2012, http://www.nytimes
   .com/2012/06/27/world/middleeast/irans-vice-president-rahimi
   -makes-anti-semitic-speech.html?_r=1&smid=tw-share, accessed July
   26, 2012.

5. Anton La Guardia, "Divine Mission Driving Iran's New Leader," January 14, 2006, http://www.telegraph.co.uk/news/worldnews/middle
   east/iran/1507818/Divine-mission-driving-Irans-new-leader.html.

6. Joel C. Rosenberg, "Why Iran's Top Leaders Believe That the End of
   Days Has Come," FoxNews.com, November 7, 2011, http://www
   .foxnews.com/opinion/2011/11/07/why-irans-top-leaders-believe-that
   -end-days-has-come, accessed July 27, 2012.

7. Joel Richardson, *Antichrist: Islam's Awaited Messiah* (Enumclaw, WA:
   Pleasant Word, 2006), 52-70.

8. Richardson, *Antichrist: Islam's Awaited Messiah*, 67-68.

9. David R. Reagan, "The Antichrist: Will He Be a Muslim"?, www
   .prophezine.com/.../TheAntichristWillhebeaMuslim/.../Default.aspx.

10. Richardson, *Antichrist: Islam's Awaited Messiah*, 198.

11. Charles Dyer and Mark Tobey, *The ISIS Crisis: What You Really Need to
    Know* (Chicago: Moody, 2015), 95.

Chapter 7—What Will Happen to America?

1. Glenn Beck, April 2009.

2. John F. Walvoord, *The Nations in Prophecy* (Grand Rapids: Zondervan
   Publishing House, 1967), 175.

3. Charles C. Ryrie, *The Best Is Yet to Come* (Chicago: Moody, 1981),
   109-10.

4. *World*, March 22/29, 2008, 18. This statistic comes from a report by the Centers for Disease Control and Prevention.

5. Jeffrey M. Jones, "Americans' Outlook for U.S. Morality Remains Bleak: Three-quarters say moral values in U.S. are getting worse," May 17, 2010, in *The Gallup Poll: Public Opinion 2010* (Lanham: Rowman & Littlefield Publishers, Inc., 2011), 162.

6. From a letter Thomas Macauley wrote on May 23, 1857 to Henry S. Randall of New York, the author of *The Life of Jefferson*.

7. Michelle Schuman, "Is the Almighty Dollar Doomed?," *Time*, April 6, 2009, http://www.time.com/time/business/article/0,8599,1889588,00.html, accessed July 30, 2012.

8. Rich Miller and Simon Kennedy, "G-20 Shapes New World Order with Lesser Role for U.S. Markets," *Bloomberg*, April 3, 2009, http://www.bloomberg.com/apps/news?pid=newsarchive&sid=axEnb_LXw5yc, accessed July 30, 2012.

9. Nick Gillespie, "News Flash: Entitlement Spending Grows Like Giant Cancer on U.S. Economy," January 25, 2010, reason.com/blog/2010/01/25/news-flash-entitlement-spending, accessed July 30, 2012.

10. Niall Ferguson, "An Empire At Risk," *Newsweek*, December 7, 2009, 44.

11. Ferguson, "An Empire At Risk," 44.

12. Ferguson, "An Empire At Risk," 42, 44.

13. Ferguson, "An Empire At Risk," 44.

14. Mona Charen, "Hardly a Friend to Israel," *The Daily Oklahoman*, May 25, 2011, 11.

15. Ben Feller, "Face to face, Netanyahu rejects Obama on borders," Associated Press, May 21, 2011, http://www.timesfreepress.com/news/2011/may/21/face-face-netanyahu-rejects-obama-borders, accessed July 30, 2012.

16. Charen, "Hardly a Friend to Israel," 11.

Chapter 8—The Coming Middle East Peace

1. See http://www.brainyquote.com/quotes/authors/d/david_bengurion
   .html#cZ3uZ757SvsGBo4t.99, accessed July 30, 2012.

2. "Poll: More than half of Egyptians want to cancel peace treaty with
   Israel," The Associated Press, April 26, 2011, http://www.haaretz.com/
   news/diplomacy-defense/poll-more-than-half-of-egyptians-want-to-
   cancel-peace-treaty-with-israel-1.358107, accessed July 30, 2012.

3. This chart was also used in Mark Hitchcock, *2012, the Bible, and the
   End of the World* (Eugene, OR: Harvest House Publishers, 2009), 144.

4. Charles H. Dyer, *World News and Bible Prophecy* (Wheaton, IL: Tyndale House Publishers, 1995), 214.

5. "Survey: 64% want Temple rebuilt," Ynetnews.com, July 30, 2009,
   http://www.ynetnews.com/articles/0,7340,L-3754367,00.html.

Chapter 9—The Times of the Signs

1. John F. Walvoord, *The Nations in Prophecy* (Grand Rapids: Zondervan
   Publishing House, 1967), 6.

2. These examples are taken from "Travel Humor," http://csswebs.com/
   Humor/Travel.asp. Greg Laurie, *Signs of the Times* (Dana Point, CA:
   Kerygma Publishing, 2011), 21-22.

3. John Walvoord with Mark Hitchcock, *Armageddon, Oil, and Terror*
   (Wheaton, IL: Tyndale House Publishers, 2007).

Chapter 10—Do Not Let Your Heart Be Troubled

1. Franklin Delano Roosevelt, quoted in James Montgomery Boice, *The
   Last and Future World* (Grand Rapids: Zondervan Publishing House,
   1974), 1-2.

2. See "The Beauty of Humility," http://stmaryvalleybloom.org/homily-
   22sunday-c.html.

3. Charles Dyer, *World News and Bible Prophecy* (Wheaton, IL: Tyndale
   House Publishers, 1995), 270.

Appendix 1: The Persia Prophecies

1. Many contemporary scholars reject the unity of the book and Isaiah's authorship of this section of the prophecy. They believe it was written by someone other than Isaiah after Cyrus had already risen to power. For a concise defense of the unity of Isaiah, see Geoffrey W. Grogan, "Isaiah," in *The Expositor's Bible Commentary*, gen. ed. Frank E. Gaebelein, vol. 6 (Grand Rapids: Zondervan Publishing House, 1986), 6-11.

2. Alfred Martin, *Isaiah: The Salvation of Jehovah* (Chicago: Moody Press, 1956), 76-77.

Appendix 2—Is Syria About to Be Destroyed?

1. This quote is popularly attributed to the former secretary of state for the U.S., Henry Kissinger.

2. Khaled Yacoub Oweis, "Assad holds Syria army despite Sunni-Alawite divide," April 6, 2011 (www.reuters.com/article/2011/04/06/us-syria-army-idUSTRE73543X20110406).

3. Mitchell Bard, "Potential Threats to Israel: Syria," February 24, 2011 (www.jewishvirtuallibrary.org/jsource/Threats_to_Israel/Syria.html).

4. "IAEA: Syria site was 'very likely' an atom reactor," Reuters (May 24, 2011).

5. Bard, "Potential Threats to Israel: Syria."

6. Edmund Sanders, "Israel fears the alternative if Syria's Assad falls," *Los Angeles Times*, March 30, 2011 (www.latimes.com/news/nationworld/world/la-fg-israel-syria-20110331,0,2764120.story?).

7. "Isaiah 17: Destruction of Damascus." www.raptureready.com/featured/gillette/Isaiah_17.html.

8. Some point to the king of the north in Daniel 11:40-45 as a reference to Syria in the end times since earlier in Daniel 11 the king of the north is the Seleucid Empire that was centered in Syria (Daniel 11:5-35). While that is possible, I believe the king of the north in Daniel 11:40 is the northern alliance of nations in Ezekiel 38, led by Russia. Ezekiel and Daniel were contemporaries, and I believe they are describing the same event. Also, the Seleucid Empire in the second century BC included much more than Syria. For a thorough discussion of this view, see Leon Wood, *A Commentary on Daniel* (Grand Rapids: Zondervan, 1973).